Tole Painting Lesson

Tole is French for tin. Tole painting is the method of painting on tin cans that was brought to America by European immigrants. Nowadays tole painting means painting on trees, tin cans, platters, or cloth. You may think that special paining ability is needed for tole painting, but this is not so. Don't worry if you paint outside the lines, the brush will go your way sooner or later.

Introduction on Tools

●PAINTS

❶ **Acrylic-based Water Paints.**
Waterproof after drying. Colors do not run even when moistened.

❷ **Water-based Acrylic Paint**
Adheres to ceramic, glass, or metal. Adheres tightly after baking in an oven (180 ℃ (360℉) for 30 ～ 40 minutes).

●MEDIUMS

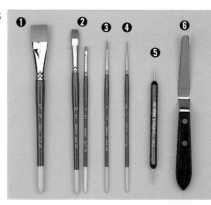

❶ **Medium for Waterproofs the base.**
Prevents absorption of the paint.

❷ **Water-based Varnish for non-glossy finish.**
Maintains condition of the craft.

❸ **Water-based Varnish for a polished finish.**
Protects and shines crafts.

❹ **Acrylic Wood Stain**
Colors and fills wood at the same time. Good for protecting exterior crafts from light and water.

❺ **Antiqued Stain, Thinner**
Oil paint for antiqued finish. Thin with paint thinner.

●BRUSHES

❶ **Flat Brush for the base (3/4"BF)**
Wide brush for painting the base. At first prepare by using 3/4" BF or 1" BF.

❷ **Flat Brush (FB)**
Mainly for painting bases, side loading, or double loading. Choose width depending on the pattern.

❸ **Round Brush (RB)**
Use these for painting comma strokes, detailed lines and patterns.

❹ **Liner Brush (LB)**
Use these for painting lines or scrolls.

❺ **Stylus**
Use to copy patterns onto Transfer paper or painting dots.

❻ **Palette Knife**
Use to mix paint.

●OTHER

❶ **Tracing Paper**
Use to copy patterns.

❷ **Transfer Paper**
Paper for transferring patterns. Transferred lines can be washed off with water.

❸ **Sandpaper (240, 400, 600, 800 grit)**
For smoothing surface of materials. Use smaller numbered paper for the base and larger numbered paper for finishing.

❹ **Tack Cloth**
Sticky paper for removing sawdust and powder from sanded surfaces. A rag can also be used.

❺ **Masking Tape**
For attaching tracing paper, or if lightly attached, for painting straight lines.

❻ **Paper Palette**
Disposable paper palette.

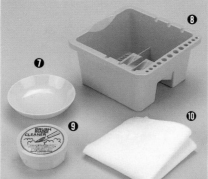

❼ **Small Bowl**
For removing medium and paint, also useful for mixing a lot of water with paints.

❽ **Brush Washer**
For washing brushes. Cups can also be used.

❾ **Brush Rinse Cleaner**
Special cleaner to make brushes last longer.

❿ **Paper Towels**
For removing excess water from brush.

Acrylic-based Water Colors

1 Safrano Pink
2 Rose
3 Claret
4 Strawberry
5 Scarlet
6 Mandarine Orange
7 Brilliant Yellow
8 Spectrum Green
9 Highland green
10 Marine Green
11 Chrome Green
12 Sky Blue

13 Pilot Blue
14 Oxford Blue
15 Dusky Purple
16 Bistre
17 Rose Wood
18 Chestnut Brown
19 Golden Brown
20 Yellow Ochre
21 Bronze Yellow
22 Vandyke Brown
23 Black
24 Livid Brown
25 Olive Gray
26 White

27 Alizarin
28 Polar Bear
29 Opaline Green
30 Sandal Wood
31 Marine Blue
32 Twilight
33 Old Rose
34 Flax
35 Magnolia
36 Burgundy
37 Niagara Green
38 Navy
39 Taupe
40 Gold

Water-based Acrylic colors

101 Magenta
102 Jack Rose
103 Orange Vermillion
104 Lemon Yellow
105 Spectrum Green
106 Pine Tree
107 Victoria Blue
108 Midnight Blue
109 Dusky Purple
110 Chestnut Brown
111 Black
112 White

● **Actual colors may vary from the printed colors.**

3

Types of Strokes and Painting

● About the types of strokes

There are two types of strokes; those made with a round brush (including a liner) and those made with a flat brush. When one color of paint is used with a round brush, it is called a comma stroke. With a flat brush it is called a broad stroke. A stroke made with two colors at the same time is called double rounding. A stroke made with paint on one side of a round or flat brush tip and water or medium on the other side is called side loading or corner loading. These are the three basic strokes. Other strokes, such as the line,scroll, or dot stroke may be added with a round or liner brush.

● Painting

It is better to practice a lot, but if you can't paint the same as the pattern, you should try to find out why. Try to paint slowly rather than quickly, which makes better strokes. In particular, take your time painting the final part of the stroke.

Comma Stroke

This is the basic stroke used in most tole painting. This can be done with a round, liner, or flat brush. (With a flat brush, it is called a broad stroke) Right now, we will concentrate on the round brush.

● With a Round Brush

Straight Comma Stroke

Right Comma Stroke

Left Comma Stroke

❶ Put paint onto the palette. Wet the tip of the brush with water, dry it with a paper towel, and then sharpen the tip of the brush.

❷ Hold the brush lightly, as you would a pen. Use the tip of the brush to draw a fine bead. Do not curve the brush.

❸ Tip the end of the brush slightly and apply pressure slowly until the tip curves. (This is where the most pressure is used.)

❹ Slowly gather the tip of the brush and raise the brush.

❺ Lift the brush until it no longer leaves a mark.

C Stroke

This can be painted with either a round (liner) brush or a flat brush.

S Stroke

This can be painted with either a round (liner) brush or by a flat brush.

● With a Round Brush

❶ Gather the tip and hold the brush as you would a pen. Concentrate on making a "C" shape and gradually apply pressure.

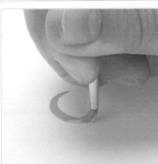

❷ When you reach the middle, remove the pressure gradually and continue.

❸ Gather the tip of the brush and raise the brush, allowing the bristles to come together. If the stroke is blurred or hazy, quickly paint it again before the paint dries out. With a Flat Brush

● With a Flat Brush

❶ Holding the brush as you would a pen, incline the brush ①. Start to gradually apply pressure before coming to point ②. Finish this way and slowly remove the pressure.

● With a Round Brush

❶ Holding the brush as you would a pen, paint while imagining an "S" shape.

❷ When you reach the middle, remove the pressure gradually and continue.

❸ Gather the brush tip and raise slowly.

● With a Flat Brush

Holding the brush as you would a pen, incline the brush and gradually apply light pressure towards position ①. Apply pressure towards position ② and continue. Remove the pressure towards position ③ and lift the tip of the brush.

● With a Flat Brush

Broad Stroke

Hold the brush vertically from the surface, paint from left to right using adequate pressure. Finish painting by lifting the brush gradually.

Right Comma Stroke

Left Comma Stroke

❶ Holding the brush as you would a pen, incline the brush and apply light pressure.
❷ Holding the brush like this, paint the stroke at an angle.
Following ②, after the curve, lift the brush gradually while painting.

Side Loading

Use this for shading or highlighting. Either a flat or round brush may be used, but a flat brush is usually used.

❶ Put water on the palette and then transfer water from the back of the brush to a spot a short distance from the paint.

❷ Moisten the flat brush and dry it with a paper towel. Touch the corner of the brush into the paint.

❸ Rotate the brush and touch the opposite corner into the water.

❹ Place the tip of the brush on the other half of the palette and stroke left and right. A gradation appears after 2 or 3 strokes.

❺ After the gradation appears, paint on the material.

Double Loading

Combine two colors in the same way as in side loading.

❶ Refer to Step ② of Side Loading. Put two colors of paint on the palette and tip one corner of the brush into one color of paint and the opposite corner into the other color.

❷ Refer to step ④ of Side Loading. Touch the brush onto the other half of the palette and stroke left and right, mixing the colors in the middle but leaving two colors at the sides.

❸ Paint on the material

Line

Any type of line; large, medium, or fine can be painted. Simply select whatever brush may be necessary; liner, round, or flat brush. In this book a liner brush is usually used.

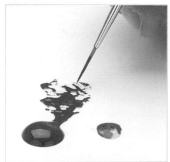

❶ Put paint and water onto the tip of the brush and straighten out the tip on the palette.

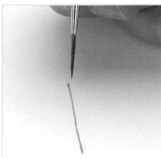

❷ Place your little finger on a flat surface and paint the line moving very smoothly.

Scroll

This may be used for flowers or veins on trees.

This is done the same way as the line. Hold the brush vertical on the flat side and move the tip of the brush only back and forth and paint.

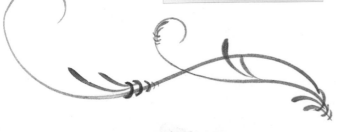

Dot

Used for flowers, centers of flowers, or bear eyes.
In this method, paint is placed on the back end of the brusu or stylus. Use a thick or thin brush depending on the purpose.

❶ Put paint on the palette and, holding the brush vertically upside-down, touch into the paint carefully. (Do not use water!)

❷ Paint holding the brush vertically.

❸ Use different sizes of brushes depending on the project.

7

Let's Make a Welcome Plaque

'

After practicing the basic strokes, master them while you make this craft. Once you've done this you'll want to tole paint all the time.

● **Tools and Materials**

Arch-shaped sign board 45.7cm×17.8cm (18" × 7")

Aclylic-based Water Paints
  Marine Green (10), Chestnut Brown(18), Vandyke Brown(32), Opaline Green(29), Sandalwood(30), Marine Blue(31), Buegundy(36),

Medium for waterproofs the base
Water-based Varnish for non-grossy finish
Brushes, 3/4" BF, FB, RB, LB
Tooth Brush
Sandpaper #400, #600, Tack Cloth, Tracing Paper, Transfer Paper, Paper Palette, Stylus, Palette Knife, Masking Tape,Washer, Small Plate Paper Towels, Pencil, etc.

1 Preparations

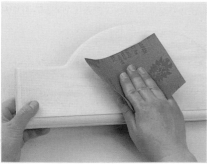

❶ Sand wood with #400 sandpaper till smooth. Remove sawdust with tack cloth.

❷ Mix equal amounts of medium for waterproofs the base and water and use a 3/4" BF to spread onto the wood following the grain.

❸ After drying, sand once more with #400 sandpaper and wipe off the sawdust. Repeat steps ② and ③ until the wood is smooth.

2 Painting

❶ Add water to parchment paint to make the proper consistency and paint this onto the wood with the 3/4" BF. (It is best if the wood can be seen clearly after the first coat.)

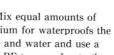

❷ Paint again after completely drying. Paint two or three times until the color is even.

❸ After drying, sand with #600 sandpaper. The brush will move smoot

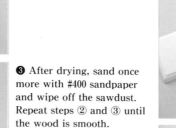

3
Framing

❶ Mix Marine Blue and Opaline Green paint (1:2) on small plate.

❷ Add sufficient water to paint from step ①. Paint lightly onto the side so that it is clear.

4 Transferring the Pattern

❶ Trace the pattern from page 58 onto tracing paper. Place the pattern onto the center of the wood, insert the Transfer Paper between them and trace the pattern with the stylus.

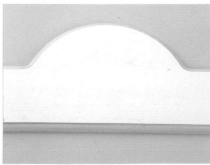

❷ Transferring is finished. (It is not necessary to copy details such as the cross pattern inside the border, because this will be done in a different color.

❸ Finished natural-grain wood. Dry sufficiently and paint. (In this picture, light oak was used. There are six other colors, such as natural wood charcoal, etc.)

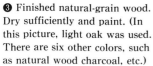

5 Border

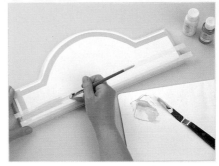

❶ Mix paints in the same proportions as in Part 3 Painting. Paint the border with a FB. Place masking tape on both sides of the straight line. Be careful not to go over the line when painting curved parts. Add a small amount of water if the brush does not move smoothly.

❷ After completely drying, trace the pattern from the Transfer Paper onto the wood. Add a sufficient amount of water to Opaline Green paint. Draw all the lines on one side with a FB, after this dries, paint the lines on the other half.

● Painting (For Stain)

This is a method for emphasizing the grain of the wood. There are two methods for doing this. One is in Painting on Page 8, and the other is the Wood Grain Method. There are two types of this, one is for water-based paint and the other is for oil-based paint.

Water-based paint dries quickly (10~30 minutes). Oil dries very slowly (half a day to one day) but it has the characteristics of the wood. Here we will introduce water-based painting. Water-based painting uses the same methods as antiquing.

❶ Using a flat brush, thickly paint wood that was sanded earlier with #400 sandpaper with acrylic wood stain. (If a lighter color is desired, add water. If a darker color is desired, do not add water.)

❷ After 30~60 seconds, wipe with a cloth. (washed cotton, etc.)

[Flower]

❽ Paint the base with Sandalwood using a FB.

[Leaf]

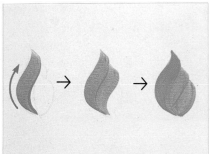

❸ Base color should be a 1:2:4 mixture of Marine Green, Vandyke Brown and Opaline Green Paint an S stroke from the bottom to the top of the leaf with a FB. Paint in two or three strokes, depending on leaf shape.

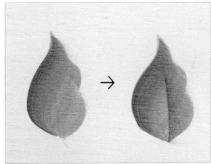

❹ Prepare a 1:3mixture of Marine Green and Vandyke Brown. Paint the center and one side of the leaves by side loading with a FB.

❾ Paint once more after drying. After this dries, trace the buds and whorls using Transfer Paper.

❺ Using Opaline Green paint highlights and accents.

Highlight   Accent

❿ Prepare a 1:1mixture of Burgundy and Chestnut Brown and shade the left side of the buds and whorls by side loading using a FB.

❻ Paint veins and edges of leaves using an LB. Paint edges of leaves with a comma stroke, and paint veins with paint thinned with water.

⓫ Shade the right side of the buds and whorls by side loading with Opaline Green using a FB.

⓬ Shade the left side and highlight the right side with comma strokes using an RB.

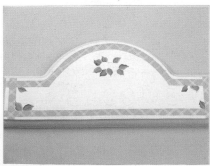

❼ Painting is finished. The leaves should not be completed one by one, but painted at one time.

⓭ Paint five or six dots at the center of flower using the wide end of the stylus.

⓮ Paint around the leaves with S and comma strokes in the same color as the base using an RB.

⓯ Add a bit of water to the same color as in step ② and paint scrolls using an LB.

[Letters]

⓰ Paint letters in Vandyke Brown with comma, S, and C strokes using an RB.

6 Fly Specking

⓱ Apply a 2:1 mixture of Marine Blue and Opaline Green mixed with a small amount of water to a toothbrush and sprinkle on the plaque by rubbing the toothbrush bristles with a stick.

7 Shadow

⓲ Paint shadows on both sides of the border with Vandyke Brown mixed with a small amount of Opaline Green using a FB. Paint the vertical bars first, then the horizontal bars. After drying paint the horizontal lines, being careful not to cross the vertical lines.

8 Completion

⓳ After completely drying, use a 3/4" BF to spread on one or two coats of Water-based Varnish.

●Antiquing

After completing a craft, it can be artificially aged to look 50~100 years older. This technique is necessary in tole painting.

❶ Mix well equal amounts of Vandyke Brown Antiqued Stain and Thinner.

❷ Spread out evenly using a flat base brush or cloth.

❸ Wipe off uneven areas and spaces with a cloth. (to make it look older, do not wipe off all of the stain.) Dry completely; at least one day, being careful not to leave fingerprints. Apply a coat of finish when dried.

II

Instructions on page 58

A planter for cute
mini-roses and margaret
that uses subdued colors,
so it can be used for both
foliage or flowers.
The same roses are
painted on the small
bucket and the mailbox.

● Floral Planter

● Small Bucket / Sample Craft

WELCOME TO THE ROSE GARDEN

Use a metal mailbox. The roses
stand out well against Dark Green.

Instructions on page 57

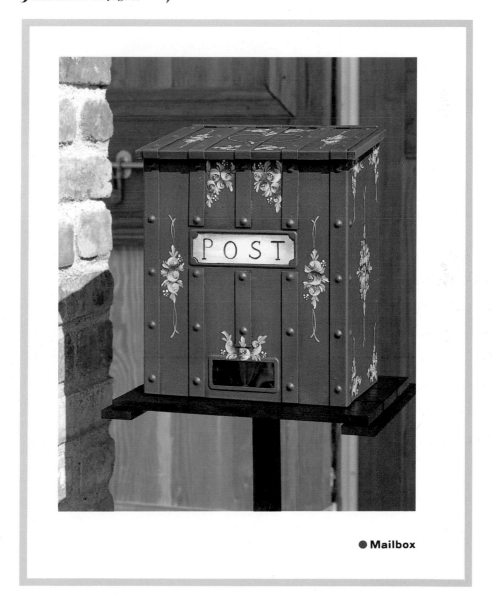

● Mailbox

Details of crafts on pages 12 and 13. [Actual Size]

Colors differ from original colors because of antiquing.

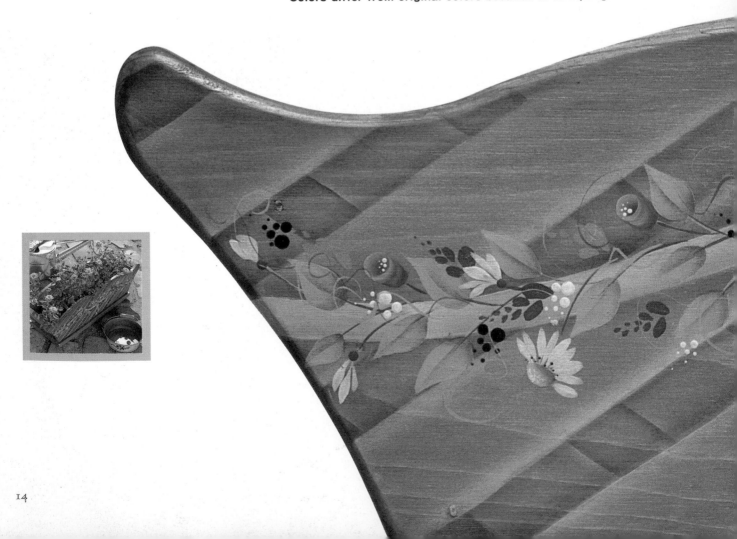

Instructions on page 61

Poppies and daisies
wrapped in a gold ribbon.
The big blossoms look
difficult at first, but need
only basic strokes. They're easy!

COZY LIVING

You'll use
them a lot, so make
them well.

● Table Cloth and Cushion

● Memo Holder ● Tissue Box

Instructions

Memo Holder on page 65
Tissue Box on page 64

Details of crafts on pages 16 and 17.
[Actual Size]

BREAKFAST IN PARIS

Three happy customers emerge from a cozy restaurant in Paris. The plate has all sorts of vegetables and cookware. These use six colors made from red, yellow, and blue.

Instructions

Oval Box page 90
Plate page 88

● **Oval Box**

● Plate

La cuiller

La poêle

Le bâton

La Cuisine

Taeko·Y   Kieko·N

Detail of crafts on pages 20, 21.
[Actual Size]

La Cuisine

Taeko・Y   Kieko・N

KITCHEN PART I

●Flower Pot   ●Cracker Tray

The narrow cracker tray
is useful as a spice rack
or cutlery case.
You'll want to plant
some herbs in the flower pot
and keep it
on the window sill.

Instructions

Flower Pot on page 66
Cracker Tray on page 66

●Cutting Board   ●Oil Pot

The cutting board
and oil pot
are interesting
and functional!

Instructions
Cutting Board on page 67
Oil Pot on page 69

Detail of crafts on pages 24 and 25.
[Actual Size]

KITCHEN PART II

When painted with special paints and baked in the oven, these crafts are washable. Before baking, paint can be washed off with a damp washcloth, so don't be afraid to make mistakes! The tile can be used as a pot stand.

Instructions; Tile on page 72, Canister on page 71

● Tile   ● Canister

Why not make an original tile? Hang them on the wall for a Spanish Motif. It will be your own little gallery.

● Tile

Instructions on page 72

●**German-Style Tulip**

30

●Chicken

Detail of crafts on pages 28 and 29.
[Actual Size]

● Tulip

● Rose Moring

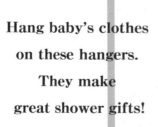

Instructions on page 70

Hang baby's clothes
on these hangers.
They make
great shower gifts!

● Hanger

FOR BABIES

This wastebasket is a
necessity for baby's room.
Baby will be cheered
every time she sees it.

Instructions on page 74

● Wastebasket

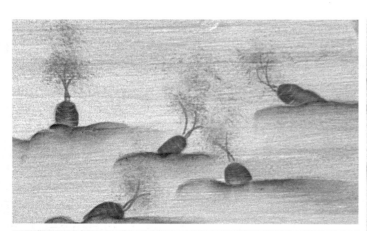

Decorated Board

Pattern size and placement are different from wastebasket on page 33.

Instructions on page 74

34

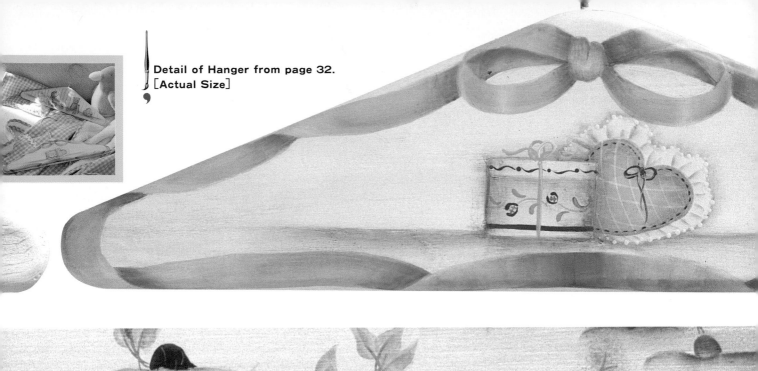

Detail of Hanger from page 32.
[Actual Size]

Noriko.Y

● Small and Large Bags

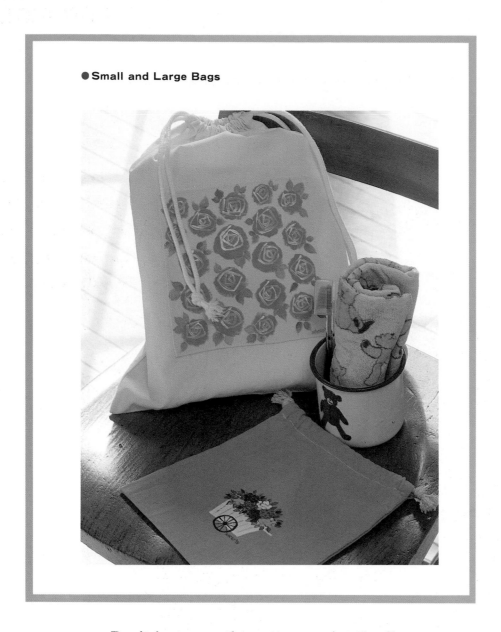

Don't just copy the pattern; paint the flowers your own way.
The painting is so easy; just paint the base and the whorls for
a warmth that you can't get from a pattern.

Instructions on page 73

●Basket

●Small Box

Three best friends
decorate the basket, and
the box shows a pretty
rose and tulip pattern.
What will you put inside?

Instructions
Basket on page 76
Small Box on page 76.

**Detail of crafts
on pages 36 and 37.
〔Actual Size〕**

NAOKO '92

FOR BOYS

Instructions

Pencil Stand on page 78
Video Game Cassette Case on page 78.

● **Pencil Stand**　　　　　　　● **Video Game Cassette Case**

The big dinosaurs make cleaning up easy. Mom's idea worked!

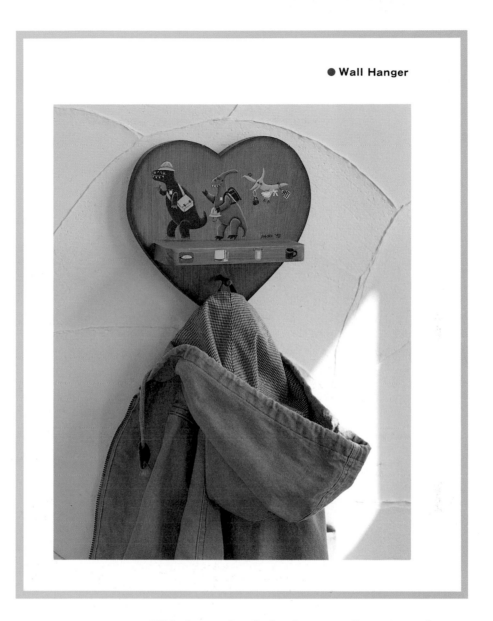

● Wall Hanger

This has a hook for bags and coats and you can put tissues or a handkerchief on the small shelf. There's no need to hurry in the morning.

Instructions on page 80

Details of crafts on pages 40 and 41.
[Actual Size]

SPINOSAURUS　スピノサウルス

FLOWERY BEDROOM

It feels so good waking up surrounded by forvorite flowers. You can use the round berry and ribbon border pattern from the pillow case for curtains, etc. The Victorian Rose stands out beautifully when the light is turned on.

Instructions

Pillow Case on page 81
Lamp Shade on page 82
Frame on page 84

● **Pillow Case**

● **Lamp Shade**

● **Frame**

Detail of crafts on pages 44 and 45.
[Actual Size]

Instructions on page 85

The Victorian rose is
painted on the paper box.
The checker pattern on
the side is an accent.

● **Gift Box**
Round Shape and Heart Shape.

GIFTS FOR YOU

The bright flowers
make this small box
just right
as a gift.

Instructions on page 88

● **Pill Box**   ● **Heart-Decoration**

Details from crafts
on page 48 and 49.
[Actual Size]

50

● **Christmas Tree**

The two of these provide a cheerful view when you're busy getting ready for Christmas.

Instructions on page 90

NOËL

House-Shaped Tissue Box   ●Decoration Board   ●Gift Can

Get ready for Christmas
by decorating
the tissue box with
forest animals and holly.

Instructions
House-Shaped Tissue Box on page 94
Decoration Board on page 92
Gift Can on page 95

Detail of crafts on page 52. [Actual Size]

MAILBOX
from page 13

●Materials and Tools

Metal Mailbox 17cm×26cm(7"×10"), 33cm(13"), tall
Acrylic-based Water Paints
　Highland Green(9),Marine Green(10), Bronze Yellow(21),Black(23),Opaline Green(29),
　Sandalwood(30),Burgundy(36),
Brushes BF、RB、LB、Stylus
Medium for Waterproofs the base
Water-based Varnish for non-glossy finish
Antiqued Stain(Burnt Amber)
Thinner

●Instructions

❶ Wipe off dirt, brush entire surface with Medium for Waterproofs the base, and dry completely.
❷ Brush Dark Green (9+23) base color over entire surface. (3/4" BF)
❸ Arrange the pattern as shown in the photo. Transfer the front and side onto the lid. (Refer to page 9)
❹ Paint each rose with 30. (RB)
❺ Shade with five of six connected C strokes using 36. Somewhat blurred is good. (RB)
❻ Paint same way with C strokes using on opposite side of step ⑤.
❼ Using the stylus, make five or six dots of 29 in the center of the flower.
❽ Paint leaves with comma strokes using Green (10+29). (RB)
❾ Highlight with 29 as in step ⑧, accent with comma strokes using 21. (Refer to photos on pages 14 and 15)
❿ Make five or six dots in the small flowers with a stylus using 29, and paint the center of flowers with 21.
⓫ Paint vertical designs above and below flower with long comma strokes in the same Green as in the leaves. (LB)
⓬ Paint center of Heart Lid with comma stroke using 29. (RB)
⓭ Antique. (Refer to page 11)
⓮ Finish up. (Refer to page 11)

[Actual Size]

WELCOME PLAQUE
from pages 1,8~11

[Actual Size]

FLORAL PLANTER
from page 12

● Materials and Tools

Wooden Planter 16.5cm×61cm(12"×24 8/3"),19cm (7 5/8")tall
Acrylic-based Water Paints
  Marine Green(10),Dusky Purple(15),Chestnut Brown(18), Bronze Yellow(21),
  Vandyke Brown(22),White(26),
  Opaline Green(29),Marine Blue(31),Burgundy(36), Niagara Green(37),
Brushes BF,FB,RB,LB,Stylus
Acrylic Wood Stain(Dark Walnut)
Water-based Varnish for non-glossy finish

● Instructions

❶ Refer to page 9 and paint with Acrylic Wood Stain. (BF)
❷ Transfer the cross pattern. (Refer to page 9)
❸ Side Load each line as in the drawing to the right with 29. To give the cross pattern perspective, shade by side loading with 22. (FB)
❹ Copy the ribbon pattern. Use a FB to paint the base with light blue (31+29). Shade as in the diagram with 31,
  and highlight by side loading with 29. (FB)
❺ Transfer the rest of the pattern.
❻ Paint the margaret flowers using comma strokes from the outside in with 29. (RB) Paint the center of the flower with 21.
  Shade with 18, and highlight by side loading with 29. (FB) After highlighting, paint dots using the tip of the brush with 26.
  Paint dots between the center of the flowers and the petals using a stylus with 22.

Comma Strokes for Flower

Noriko Yoshimura.

---

⑦ Paint the roses as in the diagram by double loading with Red = 36 + 18 and 29. (FB) Paint dots at the center of the flower with 29. (Stylus)

⑧ Paint large leaves with 37. Shade by side loading with Dark Green=10+22. (FB)

⑨ Paint the stem using the same color as the shade. (LB)

⑩ Painting small flowers with seven or eight dots using the back end of the paint brush with 29 and 15. (FB)

⑪ Paint small leaves with Yellow Green=21+37 and Dark Green = 10 + 22. Paint smaller and larger leaves alternately. (RB)

⑫ Paint stem and veins using scroll stroke with 37 and Dark Green from step ⑪. (LB)

⑬ Finish up. (Refer to page 11)

❸ **Cross**

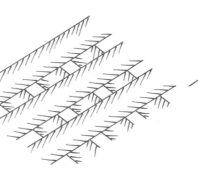

Side Loading with 29

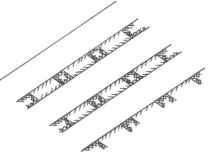

Side Loading (Shade) with 22

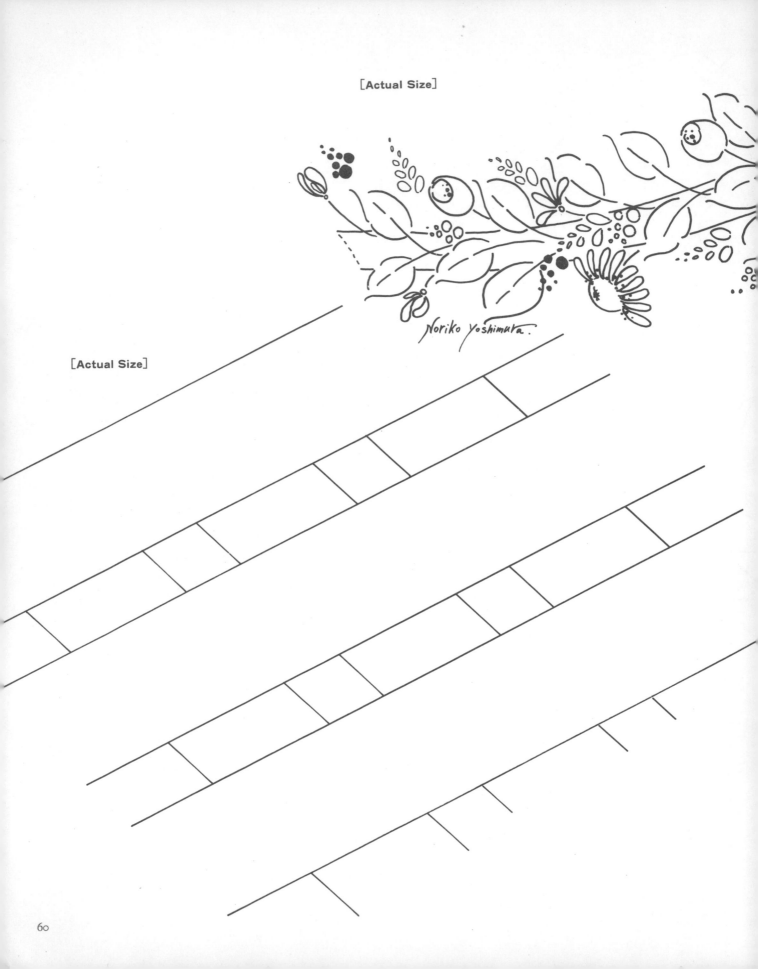

[Actual Size]

[Actual Size]

Noriko Yoshimura.

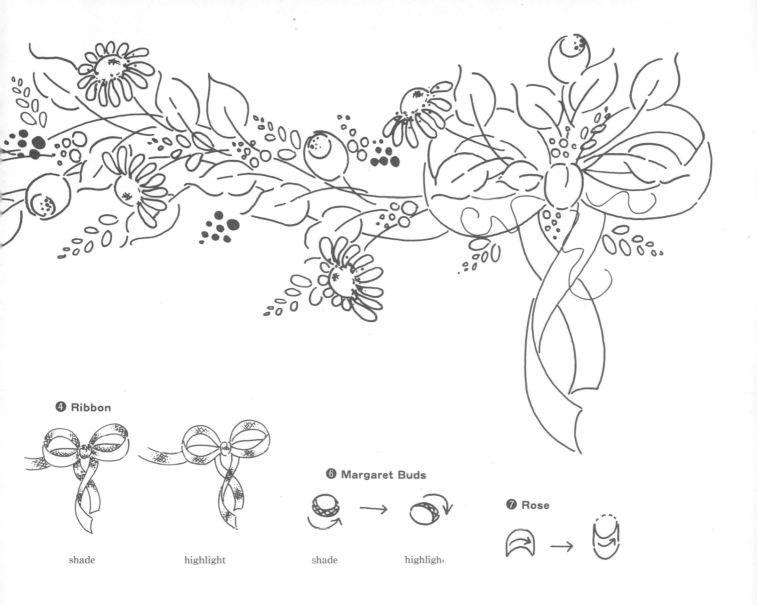

❹ Ribbon

shade　　　　　　　　highlight

❻ Margaret Buds

shade　　　　　　　highlight

❼ Rose

TABLECLOTH AND CUSHION
from page 16

●Materials and Tools

103cm (40 1/2")square Table Cloth, 40cm(16") square Cushion (can be painted without removing the stuffing)
Acrylic-based Water Paints
　Marine Green(10), Chrome Green(11), Yellow Ochre(20), Vandyke Brown(22),White(26), Opaline Green(29),
　Magnolia(35), Burgundy(36), Gold(40),
Brushes FB,RB,LB

●Instructions

❶ Transfer pattern (Refer to page 9).
❷ Paint the base for the leaves and buds using an RB with 11＋20. Paint the poppy stems with the same color (LB). Shade with 22 and
　highlight with 29. Accent tips of leaves with 20 (RB). Outline leaves and veins with 22 (LB).
❸ Use a FB to color the base for the poppies with 36＋35, and then paint around the petals by side loading the opposite side of the brush with
　26. Paint the petals by pressing an RB 20＋10. Accent with lines of 20 (LB). Use an LB with 20 and 26 to paint the stamens by making many
　dots.
❹ Paint the daisies the same as in the Tissue Box from step ⑤ on page 64.
❺ Use an RB with 40 to paint the ribbon by S and C strokes.
Paint a bouquet of poppies in each corner of the table cloth. In the middle, paint a circle of daisies 75 cm (29 1/2") in diameter.

TISSUE BOX
from page 17

● **Materials and Tools**

Wooden Tissue Box 27.5cm×14.4cm (11"×6"), 11cm (6") high.
Acrylic-based Water Paints
   Marine Green(10), Brilliant Yellow(7), Yellow Ochre(20), Vandyke Brown(22),
   Livid Brown(24), White(26),Alizarin(27), Polar Bear(28), Twilight(32), Gold(40),
Brushes BF,RB,LB,
Medium for Waterproofs the base
Water-based Varnish for non-glossy finish

● **Instructions**

❶ Prepare materials. (Refer to page 8)

❷ Paint the base using a BF with 32+28.(Refer to page 9)

❸ Transfer the pattern. (Refer to page 9)

❹ Paint the base for the leaves with a small amount of 10+32+7. Shade with by side loading with 24. (RB) Shade leaves, veins, and stems by adding a small amount of 26 to the leaf color from step ④, and paint lines. (LB)

❺ Place 20 and a lot of 26 on the RB and paint the daisy with comma strokes. Paint the center of the flowers by pressing a brush covered with 20 and then making a circle. Shade by pressing an RB covered with 22. Paint the stamen with fine lines of 26 (LB).

❻ Paint the base for the berries with 27. Shade by side loading with 22 (RB). Paint dots at the tips of the berries with 22 (LB).

❼ Paint the small flowers with the tip of a RB using 40.

❽ Finish up. (Refer to page 11)

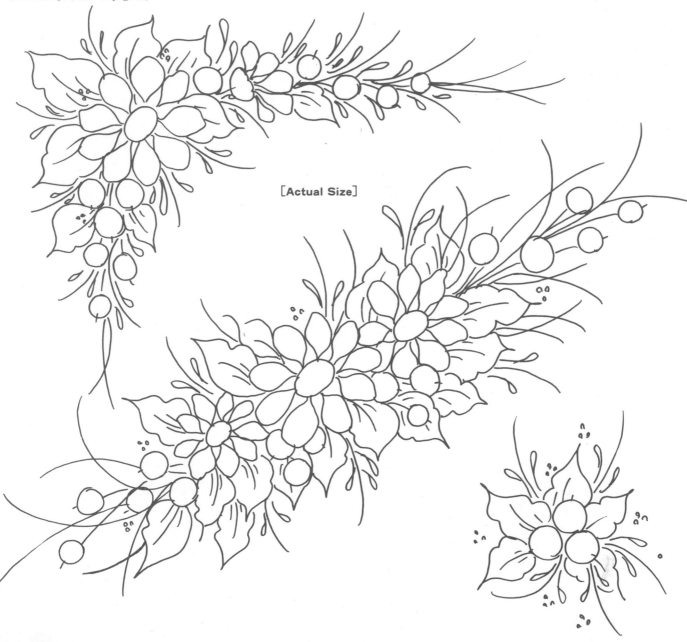

[Actual Size]

64

MEMO HOLDER

from page 17

● Materials and Tools

Wooden Message Board 26.6cm×15.2cm (10 1/2”×6”)
Acrylic-based Water Paints
  Marine Green(10), Rose Wood(17), Yellow Ochre(20),Vandyke Brown(22), White(26), Alizarin(27), Polar Bear(28),
Brushes BF,RB,LB
Medium for Waterproofs the base
Water-based Varnish for non-glossy finish

● Instructions

❶ Prepare materials. (Refer to page 8)
❷ Paint the base with a BF using 28.
❸ Transfer the pattern. (Refer to page 9).
❹ Paint all leaves in comma strokes first using 10, and then 20 on the tip of an RB. Paint the veins using 22 on an LB.
❺ Paint the base for the poppies with 27+17 using a FB. Then put 26 on one side of that brush and side load moving up and down slightly.
❻ Tap the brush on the center of the flower using 20+17 (RB). Paint the stamen with 22 and paint dots with 26 (LB). Paint the daisies with comma strokes using 20 and very much 26 (RB). Paint the center of the flower by tapping the brush in a circle 20, and shade by tapping with 22 (LB). Use a LB to paint the stamen with 26.
❼ Paint small red flowers by comma strokes with 17 using an RB. Paint the center of the flowers with 22 using an LB.
❽ Paint the petals of the small white flowers around the border using 26, the center of the flower using 20, and the stamens using 22, in the same way as for the small red flowers.
❾ Paint the wheat by making comma strokes with the tip of a brush using 20. (RB) Paint the tassels with lines of 20+22. (LB)
❿ Finish up. (Refer to page 11)

[Actual Size]

FLOWER POT
from page 24

● **Materials and Tools**

Clay Flower Pot
Acylic-based Water Paints
  Strawberry(4), Scarlet(5), Mandarine Orange(6), Marine Green(10), Pilot Blue(13), Oxford Blue(14), Chestnut Brown(18), Yellow Ochre(20),
  Livid Brown(24), White(26), Opaline Green(29), Flax(34),
Brushes BF,FB,LB,
Medium for Waterproofs the base
Water-based Varnish for non-glossy finish

● **Instructions**

❶ Brush the area to be painted with Medium for Waterproofs the base (BF).
❷ Transfer just the outside of the oval section of the pattern. (Refer to page 9) Use a BF to paint the base for the inside with 34.
❸ Side load using a FB with Orange＝6＋20 for the sky and a FB with 18 for the ground. Use the same brush to paint bumps on the ground.
❹ Transfer the pattern. Paint the walls of the house with 29, and the roof with 5 (LB). Paint the chimney and windows with 18 (LB).
❺ Lightly tap a dry brush covered with Color B＋5 to three trees on the right side. Do the same using 10＋5 to paint the trees on the left. (LB)
    After both of these have dried, tap with 18.
❻ Paint the horse and farm tools with 24 and paint a rope on the horse's waist with 19. (LB)
❼ Paint the farmer with 29, 18＋4, and 24. (LB) Paint the white in the border with 24. (LB)
❽ Paint the clouds by tapping with a dry brush dipped in 26. (LB)
❾ Paint the base for the border with Color A, Color B and 29 paint a wavy line with 29. (LB) Paint strokes outward from the center with
    Orange＝4＋14. After this has dried, paint short strokes with 13, and then paint with 29.
❿ Finish by covering with Water-based Varnish for non-glossy finish.

Color A (Blue)＝13＋24

Color B (Light Blue)＝Color A＋29

[Actual Size]

CRACKER TRAY
from page 24

● **Materials and Tools**

Wooden Cracker Tray10cm×13.4cm (4"x5 1/4"), 13.4cm (5 1/4") high
Acrylic-based Water Paints
  Scarlet(5), Spectrum Green(8), Marine Green(10), Pilot Blue(13), Chestnut Brown(18), Yellow Ochre(20), Livid Brown(24), White(26),
  Opaline Green(29), Niagara Green(37),
Brushes BF,FB,LB
Medium for Waterproofs the base
Water-based Varnish for non-glossy finish
Antiqued Stain (Chestnut Brown) and Thinner

●Instructions

❶ Prepare materials. (Refer to page 8)

❷ Paint the base with 37+5 for the outside, and 20 for the inside (BF).

❸ Transfer just the outside of the oval section of the pattern. (Refer to page 9) Paint inside this with 20 (BF).

❹ Paint waves in the upper 2/3 of the oval with Blue=13+24, and once this dries, paint outside all of the oval by side loading with 24 (FB).

❺ Paint wavy lines at the edge of the waves from step ④ with 13 (LB).

❻ Transfer the pattern. Paint the walls of the house with 29 and the roof with 5 (FB). Shade the walls with the Blue from step ④+10, the roof with the Blue from step ④+5, and highlight places where sunlight strikes the walls with 26 (FB). Paint the windows with 24 (LB).

❼ Paint tree trunks with 18, paint leaves by tapping with a dry brush with 10, finally, on top of this, tap 8+20+29 (LB).

❽ Paint house and ground by side loading a FB with 18, and paint the road with lines using the same color (LB).

❾ Paint clouds by tapping with a dry LB with 26.

❿ Paint the edge of the tray (thickness of the wood) using a dry FB with 24+5, after wiping off the excess paint.

⓫ Antique slightly. (Refer to page 11)

⓬ Finish up. (Refer to page 11)

[Actual Size]

CUTTING BOARD

from page 25

●Materials and Tools

Wooden Noodle Board 29.4cm×23cm (11 1/2"×9")

Acylic-based Water Paints

　Rose(2), Strawberry(4), Scarlet(5), Mandarine Orange(6), Spectrum Green(8), Highland Green(9), Marine Green(10), Pilot Blue(13),

Bistre(16), Chestnut Brown(18), Yellow Ochre(20), Opaline Green(29), Niagara Green(37)

Brushes BF,FB,LB,

Medium for Waterproofs the base

Water-based Varnish for non-glossy finish

●Instructions

❶ Prepare materials. (Refer to page 8)

❷ Transfer just the outside of the round section of the pattern. (Refer to page 9) Paint the base inside the circle with Light Green=37+13, and the base outside of this with 16+5. (BF)

❸ Copy the outline of the three roses and paint rough circles inside these with Red Brown=5+18. (BF)

❹ Transfer the pattern. Paint the rose petals by double loading a FB with 5+6+2, and the center of the flowers with 29 (LB).

❺ Paint the leaves as in the diagram with Blue Green=14+9+10 and Olive Green=10+18 (FB).

❻ Paint the outer edges of the board clockwise by side loading with 20 (FB).
　Paint comma strokes with the Light Green from step ② and 20 (LB).

❼ Paint motion lines around the flowers and petals with 4+14 thinned with water (LB).

❽ Finish up. (Refer to page 11)

❺ **Painting Leaves**

Bottom of leaves

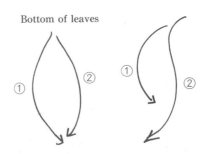

OIL POT
from page 25

●Materials and Tools

Metal Pitcher
Acrylic-based Water Paints
  Strawberry(4), Scarlet(5), Highland Green(9), Oxford Blue(14), Yellow Ochre(20), Opaline Green(29), Flax(34)
Brushes BF,FB,LB,
Medium for Waterproofs the base
Water-based Varnish for non-glossy finish

●Instructions

❶ Prepare by brushing with Medium for Waterproofs the base. (BF).

❷ Paint the base with Orange=5+20 (BF).

❸ Trace just the line surrounding the pattern of the flower (Refer to page 9). Paint inside this with Tan=34+24 (BF).

❹ Transfer the rest of the pattern. Paint the large flower in the center by double loading with 29+the Orange from the base (FB).
  Paint the center of the flower round with 29 (LB).

❺ Paint the flowers on the left and right and the buds with the Orange from the base.

❻ Paint the lower yellow leaves with 20 and the remaining green leaves one by one from the bottom with 14+9 (LB).

❼ Paint the outlines of the flower and leaves and the dots at the top and bottom of the pot with 4+14 (LB).

❽ Paint the handle, spout and the rest pattern for the front of the pot using comma strokes with 34+20,
  and the leaves on the spout with the Green from step ❻(LB).

❾ Finish by brushing twice with Water-based Varnish for non-glossy finish (BF).
  After this, bake in a 110℃ (230˚F) oven for fifteen minutes to increase strength.
  (Be careful! If the oven is too hot, it will burn).

[Actual Size]

Handle

Spout

Toy and Bears

●Materials and Tools

Wooden Hanger (Children's) 28 cm (11") wide
Acrylic-based Water Paints
  Highland Green(9), Rose Wood(17), Chestnut Brown(18), Blonze Yellow(21), Vandyke Brown(22),
  Black(23), White(26), Opaline Green(29), Marine Blue(31), Magnolia(35), Burgundy(36), Navy(38),
Brushes BF,FB,RB,LB,Stylus
Medium for Waterproofs the base
Water-based Varnish for non-glossy finish

●Instructions

❶ Prepare materials. (Refer to page 8)
❷ Paint base with 29 (BF).
❸ Transfer the pattern. (Refer to page 9)
❹ Paint the bear's face, body, arms, and legs with 21+29 (FB). Paint evenly, don't apply much paint it all at one time. Dry first, then paint again. Shade each part of the bear by side loading with 18. Side load on top of this with 22 (FB). After it dries, highlight by side loading with 29 (FB). Paint the eyes and nose with 23, and the mouth with 36 (RB). Paint dots in the eyes with 26 (Stylus).
  Paint the buttons with 36, and the neck ribbon with 38+23 on the left side, and 36 on the right side. Highlight with 29 (LB).
❺ Paint lines on the left cushion with 31 and the right cushion with 35 (LB).
  Paint the surroundings and inside by side loading with the same colors (FB).
❻ Shade by side loading on each face of the blocks with 31, and the opposite angles with 21 (FB).
  Paint the patterns on the blocks with 36, 17, and 9 (LB). Highlight by side loading with 29 (FB).
❼ Paint the bag by side loading with 31 (FB).
  Paint stitching with 29 (LB).
❽ Paint the floor by side loading with 21,
  Shade by side loading with 18 (FB).
❾ Finish up. (Refer to page 11)

[Actual Size]

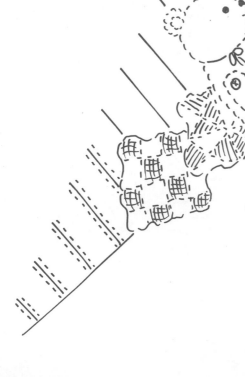

Heart Cushion and Box

●Materials and Tools

Wooden Hanger (Children's) 28 cm (11") wide
Acrylic-base Water Paints
  Marine Green(10), Chestnut Brown(18), Bronze Yellow(21), White(26),
  Polar Bear(28), Opaline Green(29), Sandalwood(30), Marine Blue(31),
  Magnolia(35), Burgundy(36),
Brushes BF,FB,RB,LB, Stylus
Medium for Waterproofs the base
Water-based Varnish for non-glossy finish

●Instructions

❶ Prepare materials. (Refer to page 8)
❷ Paint base with 29 (BF).
❸ Transfer the pattern. (Refer to page 9)
❹ Paint base for the ribbon with Light =30 (FB), and shade by side loading with Medium= 35, and Dark= 36 (FB). Make a gradation in the pink through dark, medium, and light, and highlight for more depth by side loading with 29 (FB).
❺ Paint the inside of the Heart Cushion with 31+29 (FB). Shade the inside of the heart by side loading with 31 (FB). Copy the inside of the heart and paint the cross lines with 26, and the stitches and strings with 31 (LB). Paint frills with 26. Shade by side loading with 31 (FB). Paint dots at the edge of the frill with 26 (Stylus).
❻ Paint box with 29 (FB). Dry and paint again evenly. Copy the pattern. Paint flowers, leaves, and lines at top and bottom with 36 and 10+28 with comma strokes, S strokes, and dots (RB). Paint cross lines at the center of the flower with 21 (LB). Paint ribbon with 35 (LB). Shade both sides of the box by side loading with 18 (FB).

❼ Side load the floor with 21, and shade by side loading with 18 (FB).

❽ Finish up. (Refer to page 11)

[Actual Size]

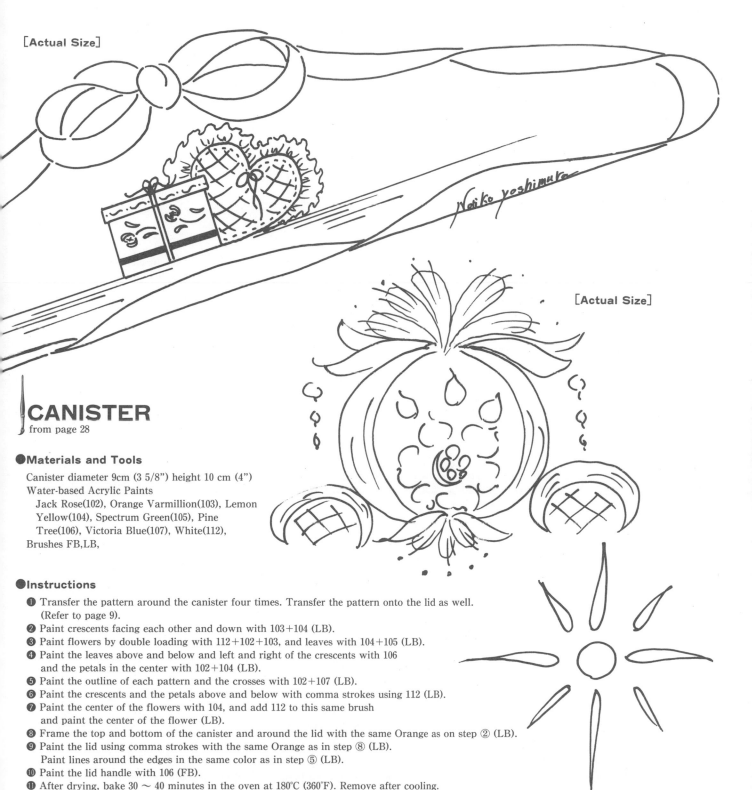

[Actual Size]

CANISTER
from page 28

● Materials and Tools

Canister diameter 9cm (3 5/8") height 10 cm (4")
Water-based Acrylic Paints
  Jack Rose(102), Orange Varmillion(103), Lemon
  Yellow(104), Spectrum Green(105), Pine
  Tree(106), Victoria Blue(107), White(112),
Brushes FB,LB,

● Instructions

❶ Transfer the pattern around the canister four times. Transfer the pattern onto the lid as well.
  (Refer to page 9).

❷ Paint crescents facing each other and down with 103+104 (LB).

❸ Paint flowers by double loading with 112+102+103, and leaves with 104+105 (LB).

❹ Paint the leaves above and below and left and right of the crescents with 106
  and the petals in the center with 102+104 (LB).

❺ Paint the outline of each pattern and the crosses with 102+107 (LB).

❻ Paint the crescents and the petals above and below with comma strokes using 112 (LB).

❼ Paint the center of the flowers with 104, and add 112 to this same brush
  and paint the center of the flower (LB).

❽ Frame the top and bottom of the canister and around the lid with the same Orange as on step ② (LB).

❾ Paint the lid using comma strokes with the same Orange as in step ⑧ (LB).
  Paint lines around the edges in the same color as in step ⑤ (LB).

❿ Paint the lid handle with 106 (FB).

⓫ After drying, bake 30 ~ 40 minutes in the oven at 180℃ (360°F). Remove after cooling.

TILE
from pages 28 and 29

German Style Tulip

●Materials and Tools

Tile 14.8 cm (5 3/4") square
Water-based Acrylic Paints
Jack Rose(102), Orange Varmillion(103), Lemon Yellow(104), Victoria Blue(107), Midnight Blue (108), Black(111), White(112),
Brushes FB,LB,

●Instructions

❶ Copy the actual size photos from page 30 and transfer onto the tile. (Refer to page 9).
❷ Paint the heart at the center and the surrounding leaves with a brush dipped in water using 107 (FB). Paint leaves outward from the center.
❸ Paint the petals outward from the center with 101+103 (FB).
❹ Paint the pedestal below the heart in layers by side loading with 102+104 (FB).
❺ Paint around the edges of the tile with the same color as in step ③ (FB).
❻ Paint the edges from step ⑤, around the hearts, and sides of the leaves using comma strokes with 107+111 (LB).
❼ Paint edges of leaves with 107+102 (LB).
❽ Add comma strokes in the heart and leaves with 112 (LB).
❾ After drying, bake 30~40 minutes in the oven at 180℃ (360˚F). Remove after cooling.

Tulip

●Materials and Tools

Tile 10.9 cm (4 1/4") square
Water-based Acrylic Paints
Magenta(101), Victoria Blue(107),
Midnight Blue(108), Black(111),
brushes FB,LB

●Instructions

❶ Copy the actual size photos from page 31 and transfer onto the tile. (Refer to page 9).
❷ Lightly paint the base for the curtains, petals, and table using a wet brush with 108 (FB).
❸ Paint the tulips as well using LB with the same color as in step ②.
❹ Paint the tulip leaves outward from the center with 107+111 (LB).
❺ Paint the outline of each pattern with 107 (LB).
❻ After drying, bake 30~40 minutes in the oven at 180℃ (360˚F). Remove after cooling.

Chicken

●Materials and Tools

Tile 10.9 cm (4 1/4") square
Wate-based Acrylic Paints
Victoria Blue(107), Midnight Blue(108), Black(111),
Brushes FB,LB

●Instructions

❶ Copy the actual size photos from page 31 and tranfer onto the tile. (Refer to page 9).
❷ Lightly paint the base for the body of the chicken using a wet brush with 108 (LB).
❸ Paint the ground, clouds and left leaves by side loading with 108 (FB).
❹ Paint the comb and legs with 107+111 (LB).
❺ Paint the decorations at the corners of the tile and chicken's tail with 107 outward from the center (LB).
❻ Paint the flower, chicken's tail, and corner dots with 108 (LB).
❼ Paint the body of the chicken, flower, cloud, and outline of the ground with 107 (LB).
❽ After drying, bake 30~40 minutes in the oven at 180℃ (360˚F). Remove after cooling.

❷ Order of painting

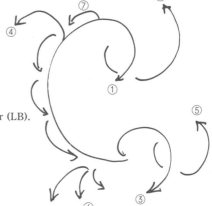

Rose Moring

●Materials and Tools

Tile 10.9 cm (4 1/4") square
Water-based Acrylic Paints
Jack Rose(102), Orange Vermillion(103), Lemon Yellow(104), Spectrum Green(105), Victoria Blue(107), Midnight Blue(108), White(112),
Brushes FB,LB

●Instructions

❶ Copy the actual size photos from page 31 and tranfer onto the tile. (Refer to page 9).
❷ Put paint onto a wet brush and paint from ①~⑦, according to the separate diagram:1~2=108(FB), 5,6=102+104 (LB), 7=104+103 (LB)
❸ Paint a circle in the Light Orange flower using a wet brush with 112+104+102 (FB).
❹ Paint leaves with 105+104 (LB).
❺ Paint corners of tile with 102+104 (FB).
❻ Paint the outlines of each pattern with 107 (LB). For the light lines use a very wet brush, and for the dark lines use a brush with less water and vary pressure on the brush.
❼ After drying, bake 30~40 minutes in the oven at 180℃ (360˚F). Remove after cooling.

LARGE AND SMALL BAGS
from page 36

from page 36

Large Bag

●Materials and Tools

Cotton; Off-White 77cm×33cm (30 1/4"×13")
Cream 18cm (7") square
0.5cm (1/4") thick Cotton Cord 75cm (30")
2 pieces
Acrylic-based Water Paints
Rose(2), White(26), Niagara Green(37),
Brushes FB,RB

●Instructions

❶ Wash and iron the cloth.
❷ Refer to the photo on page 38 and paint a base of appropriate size on the applique cloth (FB).
❸ Paint spirals with 26 (RB).
❹ Paint the leaves as in the diagram using one-stroke leaves (FB).
❺ Finish as in the diagram.

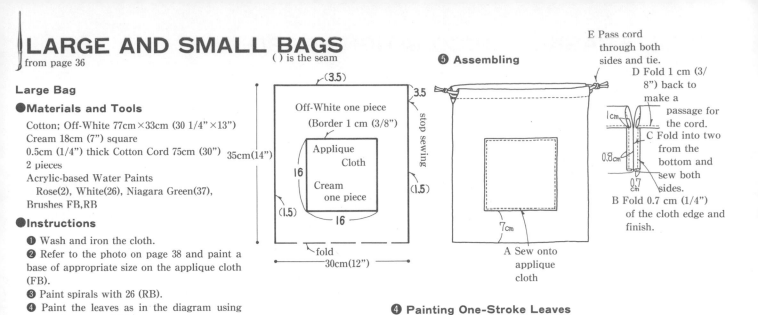

( ) is the seam

(3.5)

Off-White one piece
(Border 1 cm (3/8"))

Applique
Cloth

Cream
one piece

16

16

(1.5)

fold

30cm(12")

35cm(14")

3.5

stop sewing

(1.5)

❺ **Assembling**

E Pass cord through both sides and tie.
D Fold 1 cm (3/8") back to make a passage for the cord.
C Fold into two from the bottom and sew both sides.
B Fold 0.7 cm (1/4") of the cloth edge and finish.

1cm
0.8cm
0.7cm

7cm

A Sew onto applique cloth

❹ **Painting One-Stroke Leaves**

Start from flat brush corner and lift at opposite side.

Small Bag

●Materials and Tools

Pink Cotton 46cm×21cm (18"×8 1/4")
0.5cm(1/4") thick Cotton Cord 50cm(19 3/4") 2 pieces
Acrylic-based Water Paints
Claret(3), Strawberry(4), Mandarine Orange(6),
Marine Green(10), Dusky Purple(15),
Golden Brown(19), Vandyke Brown(22),
Black(23), Olive Glay(25), White(26),
Brushes FB,RB,LB

●Instructions

❶ Wash and iron the cloth as in Large Bag and sew as a bag.
❷ Transfer the pattern. (Refer to page 9).
❸ Paint flower wagon with 26 (FB). Paint lines with 25 and wheels with 22 (LB).
❹ Paint leaves as one stroke leaves (Refer to Large Bag) with 23 mixed with an adequate amount of 10 (FB).
❺ Paint flowers with 3, 19, 15+26, 26, 6, and 4, and paint circles with large amounts of paint. Before it dries, paint here and there with 26, 4, and 23 (RB)

( ) is the seam

(3)

One piece

20cm(8")

(1.5)

2

stop sewing

(1.5)

4

fold

18cm(7")

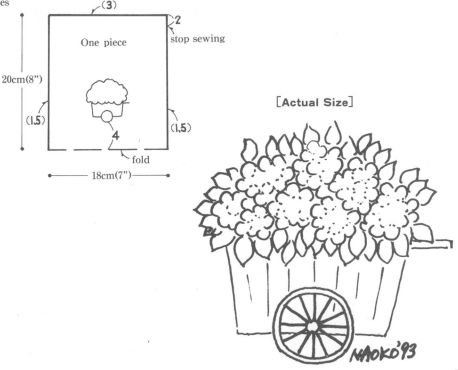

[Actual Size]

NAOKO'93

WASTEBASKET, DECORATION BOARD

from pages 33 and 34

Decoration Board

●Materials and Tools

Wooden Plaque 45 cm x 23.6 cm (17 3/4" ×9 1/4")
Acrylic-based Water Paints
 Marine Green(10), Rose Wood(17), Chestnut Brown(18),
 Bronze Yellow(21), Vandyke Brown(22), Black(23),
 White(26), Opaline Green(29), Marine Blue(31),
 Magnolia(35),Burgundy(36), Navy(38),
Brashes BF,FB,RB,LB, Stylus
Medium for Waterpsoofs the base
Water-based Varnish for non-glossy finish

●Instructions

❶ Prepare materials. (Refer to page 8)
❷ Paint base with 29 (BF).
❸ Transfer the pattern. (Refer to page 9).
❹ Paint base for the rabbit with 26, shade by side loading with 31 (FB). Paint ears, cheeks, and legs by side loading with 35 (FB). Paint the ribbon and nose the same color (RB). Paint eyes with 23＋38 (RB), and paint eyelashes the same color (LB). Put 26 on the tip of the brush and paint two dots (RB). Paint line for mustache with 21 (LB). Put 22 at the tip of the brush and paint fine dots (RB).

[Actual Size]

74

❺ Paint the staves of the vegetable basket one by one using the wide side of the brush with 21, shade by side loading with 18 (FB). Paint gaps and joints with 22 (LB). Paint the band with the same color (FB). Highlight by side loading in three places with 26 (FB).
❻ Paint the beets with 36 (FB). Shade with 22, and highlight by side loading with 29 (FB). Paint small lines on the beets with 29 (LB). Paint leaves by side loading with Green=10+22+29 (FB). Paint the stem as a line with the same color (LB).
❼ Paint the cabbage by side loading the same color as the beet leaves, shade by side loading with 10 (FB).
❽ Paint carrots with 21+29 (FB), and side load both sides with 17 (FB). Paint small lines with 29, and paint stem the same color as the beet leaves (LB). Paint leaves by wiping extra paint off of dry brush and tapping paint onto the leaves (FB). In the same way, tap 26 on top of this.
❾ Paint grass as lines using the same green as the beet leaves mixed with 10 (LB). Paint dots of 36 (Stylus).
❿ Paint the piles of soil and the lower part of the picture by side loading with 21+29, shade by side loading with 18 (FB).
⓫ Finish up. (Refer to page 11)

Wastebasket

●Materials and Tools

Wastebasket opening diameter 22cm (8 3/4"),
death 28cm(11")
Other materials same as Decoration Board.

●Instructions

Brush base with Medium for waterproofs the base. Paint the upper and lower 3～4cm (1 1/4" ～ 1 1/2") with 38 + 23 + 22. Make in the same way as the Decoration Board. Size and placement of pattern should be changed for balance.

Noriko Yoshimura

SMALL BOX
from page 37

●Materials and Tools

Wooden Box (Recipe Box) 14.8cm×9.8cm (5 3/4"×3 3/4") height 9.8cm (3 3/4")
Acrylic-based Water Paints
 Safrano Pink(1), Strawberry(4), Marine Green(10),
 Chrome Green(11), Oxford Blue(14),
 Dusky Purple(15), White(26), Burgundy(36),
Brushes BF,FB,RB,LB, Saylus
Medium for Waterproofs the base
Water-based Varnish for non-glossy finish

●Instructions

❶ Prepare materials. (Refer to page 8)

❷ Paint base for all except sides of lid with 26, paint sides of lid and inside with 11 (BF).

❸ Side load the edges of the white part with 11 (FB).

❹ Copy only the outside of the oval pattern onto the lid. Paint inside the lid with 1 (FB). Side load inside the outline with 26, and outside the outline with 11 (FB).

❺ Paint comma strokes on top of the side loading with 26 (LB).

❻ Transfer the lid pattern. (Refer to page 9)

❼ Paint the base for the roses with Pink＝4+26 (1:1). Double load with Pink and White and paint petals on the far side and then the near side, and paint the two sides of the rose on the bottom with comma strokes by double loading (FB).

❽ Paint rose buds with Pink by side loading to the bottom with 4 (FB).

❾ Paint symmetrical tulips with two S strokes with 14＋26 (1:1) and shade by side loading both sides with 15 (FB).

❿ Paint cockscomb with 36 (LB).

⓫ Paint leaves with S strokes, and one-stroke leaves (refer to page 73) using Green＝10+26 (1:1) (FB). Paint small surrounding leaves with RB. Paint dots in the center and the surrounding area with 26 and 36 (Stylus).

⓬ Transfer the pattern onto the sides and paint comma strokes in the same Green as the leaves (LB).

⓭ Finish up. (Refer to page 11)

Lid

[Actual Size]

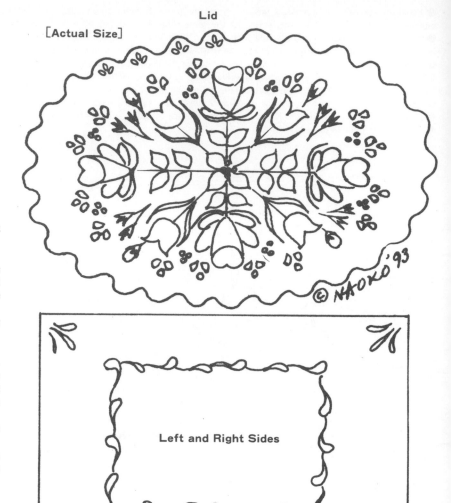

© NAOKO '93

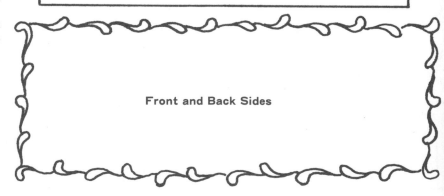

Left and Right Sides

Front and Back Sides

BASKET
from page 37

●Materials and Tools

Oval Wooden Basket 18.6cm×26cm (7 1/4"×10 1/4"), depth 15.6cm (6 1/4")
Acrylic-based Water Paints
 Safrano Pink(1), Scarlet(5), Highland green(9), DuskyPurple(15), Bistre(16), Chestnut Brown(18),
 Golden Brown(19), Bronze Yellow(21), Vandyke Browm(22), Black(23), Olive Gray(25), White(26),
 Polar Bear(28), Burgandy(36), Niagara Green(37)
Brushes BF,FB,RB,LB Stylus
Medium for Waterproofs the base
Water-based Varnish for non-glossy finish

●Instructions

❶ Prepare materials. (Refer to page 8)

❷ Transfer only the oval pattern onto the middle of the front of the basket. (Refer to page 9)

❸ Paint base on sides and handle with 36, paint edges of sides and handle with 28, and inside with 9 (BF).

❹ Paint girls and fox as in separate table.

❺ Paint lines on edges with 25+23 (1:1) (RB), and fine lines with 36 (LB).

❻ Side load around the outside of the oval with 23 (FB). ⸎

❼ Finish up. (Refer to page 11)

Color Matching and Painting for step ❹

B means the base color (FB)
S means shade by side loading (FB)
H means highlight by side loading (FB)
Paint lines or details with Liner Brush.

Same

Girl's Faces, Arms, Legs
B=1+small amount of 18 S=18
Fox's Face, Arms, Legs B=21+26 S=22
Jacket, Collar, Socks B=26 S=25
Stitches on Jacket, Lines on Socks 25
Girls' Shoes B=23 H=26
Fox's Shoes B=36 S=36+23
Eyes, Fox's Nose B=23 Dot=26
Girls' Eyebrows, Noses 18
Cheeks, Girls' Mouths36 to paint cheeks, use a dry round brush with paint, wipe off excess, and tap

Girl on Left

Hair B=16 Line=18
Ribbon, Pattern on Jacket 15+26
Skirt B=37 S=37+23
Doll's Dress 5
Doll's Hair 19+26

Girl on Right

Hair B=18 Line=22
Hair Band 23
Skirt B=36 S=36+23
Letter on Jacket, Doll's Skirt and Shoes 15+26
Doll's Hair 19+26
Heart on Socks 36

Fox

Hair Band B=36 S=23 H=26
Dress B=5 S=18 Dot=26
Whiskers 16
Basket 36

[Actual Size]

© NAOKO '93

PEN HOLDER

from page 40

●Materials and Tools

Wooden Pencil Holder 12cm×17.7 (4 3/4" × 7"),
height 16.7cm(6 1/2")
Acrylic-based Water Paints
 Strawberry(4), Marine Green(10), Dusky Purple(15),
 Golden Brown(19), Black(23), White(26),
Brushes BF,FB,RB,LB, Stylus
Acrylic Wood Stain(Light Oak)
Water-based Varnish for non-glossy finish

●Instructions

❶ Refer to page 9 and brush with Acrylic Wood Stain (BF).
❷ Paint front, back, and inside (except for both sides and the thickness of the wood) Green=10+26 (1:1) (BF).
❸ Transfer the outline of the oval onto the back and front (refer to page 9). Paint inside with 26 (BF).
❹ Trace the dinosaur and paint the same Green as the base in step ②, shade by side loading with the base color+23 (FB). Paint fin, paws, and legs with 4. Paint fin bones by side loading with 4+23 (FB). Paint eyes and teeth with 26 (RB). Paint outline and pupils with 23 (LB). Paint pencil and ruler with 15+26 and 23 (LB). Paint body pattern with 19, 4, 15+26 (RB). Paint cheeks by tapping with a dry brush with 4 after wiping off the excess.
❺ Paint around the oval, the stitches, and the letters with 23 (LB).
❻ Paint diamonds around the handle with 4 (RB), and the dots with the same purple as in step ④ (Stylus).
❼ Refer to page 43 and paint the stamps on both sides in the same way as the dinosaurs. Paint cheeks of dinosaurs above and below with Pink=4+26.
❽ Finish up. (Refer to page 11)

VIDEO GAME CASSETTE BOX

from page 40

●Materials and Tools

Enpty Can 23.5cm×23.5 (9 1/4" × 9 1/4"), depth 17cm(6 3/4")
Acrylic-based Water Paints
 Strawberry(4), Marine Green(10), Chrome Green(11), Golden Brown(19), Black(23), Olive Gray(25), White(26), Opaline Green(29),
 Burgundy(36), Navy(38),
Brushes BF,FB,RB,LB, Stylus
Medium for Waterproofs the base
Water-based Varnish for non-glossy finish

●Instructions

❶ Remove dust from can, brush with Medium for Waterproofs the base (BF).

❷ Paint entire outside of can with 29 (BF). Do not paint part of the can where lid overlaps.

❸ Paint 1.5～2cm (5/8"～3/4") of the each edge with Navy Blue=38+23 (1:2) (BF).

❹ Transfer the pattern of the dinosaur playing the video game onto the front and back and dinosaur only onto the sides. (Refer to page 9)

❺ Refer to separate table and paint.

❻ Paint triangles on each corner of the lid with 18, and paint dots using the back side of the brush with 38+26, 4, 19, 10+19.

❼ Paint checker pattern on lid with the Dark Blue from step ❸ (BF). After it dries, side load on one side with 23 (FB).

❽ Paint lines on edges of border and checker pattern with 29 (LB).

❾ Finish up. (Refer to page 11)

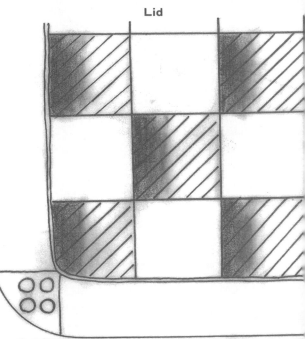

Lid

Color Matching and Painting for Step ❺

B means the base color (FB)
S means shade by side loading (FB)
H means highlight by side loading (FB)
Paint lines or details with Liner Brush

TV

Front Edge of TV B=Navy Blue from step ❸+26 H=26

Top of TV B=Navy Blue from step ❸ H=26

Sides and Base of TV B=Navy Blue from step ❸+23

Backside of TV and Antenna B=23

TV Screen B=25+26 (1:1) S=23

Body of Dinosaur B=10 S=23

Stomach, Saddle, Eye B=26

Paws, Shoes, Fins, Mushrooms, Edges of Saddle B=4

Coins, Base of Mushroom B=19

Video Game Player

Top, Controller B=25+26

Sides   B=25

Start Button, Plug B=23

Front of Cassette B=19+26

Sides of Cassette, Top B=19

Dinosaurs on Left and Right

Body of Left Dinosaur, Arms, Legs, and Fins of Right Dinosaur B=4 S=36

Body of Right Dinosaur, Arms, Legs, and Fins of Left Dinosaur B=10+26 S=11

Eyes, Teeth 26 Pupils 23

Cheeks Left 4+26 Right use a dry round brush with 4, wipe off excess, and tap.

All Outlines, Cord, Antenna 23

[Actual Size]

© NAOKO '93

WALL HANGING
from page 41

● Materials and Tools

Wooden Wall Hanger (remove the house from the house with a heart) 22cm×22.5cm (8 3/4"×9")
Acrylic-based Water Paints
   Marine Green(10), Golden Brown(19), Vandyke Brown(22), Black(23), Olive Gray(25), White(26), Polar Bear(28), Burgundy(36)
Brushes BF,FB,RB,LB,Stylus
Acrylic Wood Stain(Light Oak)
Water-based Varnish for non-Glossy finish

● Instructions

❶ Refer to page 9 and brush with Acrylic Wood Stain (BF).
❷ Paint around the heart by side loading with 22, paint the same color onto the thickness of the wood (FB).
❸ Refer to separate table and paint.
❹ Finish up. (Refer to page 11)

Color Matching and Painting for Step ❸

B means the base color (FB)
S means shade by side loading (FB)
H means highlight by side loading (FB)
Paint lines or details with Liner Braush.

Dinosaur on Left

Body B=36 S=36+23
Arms and Legs B=36 S=36+23
Bag B=28 S, Buckle=22

Dinosaur in Middle

Body B=10 S=10+23
Arms and Legs B=36 S=36+23
Satchel B=23 Strap=28

Dinosaur
  on Right

Body B=19 S, Breast=22
Apron, Bag B=26 Outline=25 Plaid
on Bag=36
Cup B=36 S=36+23

Same

School Caps B=19 S=22
Eyes, Teeth 26 Pupils 23
Straps on Caps, Outlines of Eyes and
Teeth 23
Cheeks Left 36+26,
Right and Inside; use a dry round brush
with 36, wipe off excess, and tap

Small Items

Tissues B=10 S=10+23
Paper and Stitches 26
Handkerchief B=26 S=23 Lines=36
Name Tag Inside = 26 Edge = 19
Safety Pin=25+23 S=22
Cup B=36 S=23

[Actual Size]

© NAOKO '93

PILLOW CASE
from page 44

●Materials and Tools

Pillow Case
Acrylic-based Water Paints
   Highland Green(9), Marine Green(10), Sky Blue(12), Dusky Purple(15), Yellow Ochre(20), White(26),
Burgundy(36), Niagara Green(37), Navy(38)
Brushes FB,Stylus

●Instructions

❶ Wash and iron the pillow case.
❷ Transfer the pattern continuously. (Refer to page 9)
❸ Refer to the diagram and paint the berries, ribbon, and leaves.

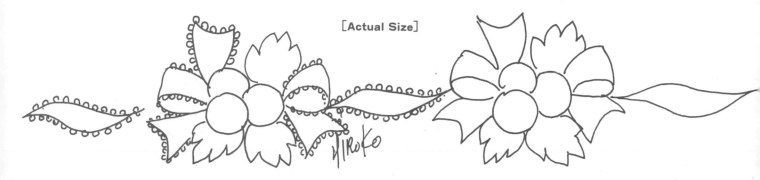

[Actual Size]

Color Matching and Painting for step ❸

Berry

 → →

Medium 36   Light 26   Highlight 12＋37＋26

Side Loading (FB)

Paint the berries based on a pink cloth. If the color of the base is different, paint the base pink.

Ribbon

 →  → →

Base FB 12＋37＋26   Shade 15   Highlight 26   Dot 26 (Stylus)

Side Loading (FB)

Leaf

 → → →

Base 10＋26 (FB)   Dark 9   Shade 9＋38   Highlight 12＋37＋26

Side Loading (FB)

LAMP SHADE

from page 45

●Materials and Tools

Lamp Shade with Black Cloth
Acrylic-based Water Paints
  Safrano Pink(1), Highland Green(9), Marine Green(10), Dusky Purple(15), Bistre(16), Yellow Ochre(20), Bronze Yellow(21), Black(23),
  White(26), Opaline Green(29), Burgundy(36), Gold(40)
Brushes BF,FB,LB, Stencil Brush(Fine)

●Instructions

❶ Transfer the pattern four times. (Refer to page 9)
❷ Paint by side loading, the top and bottom with 23, border between colors with 16, top and bottom edges of lamp shade with 26 (BF).
❸ Paint the border between colors using comma strokes with 40 (RB).
❹ Paint roses and leaves in order as in the separate section.
❺ To make the bouquet, overlap 36 and 26 onto the stencil brush and tap on the position. On top of this, paint tiny flowers with 26 using the corner of a flat brush. Make S strokes around the flowers by double loading with 10 and 26 (FB).
❻ Join the bouquet and roses by painting comma strokes with the same color as the leaves in step ⑤ (RB).

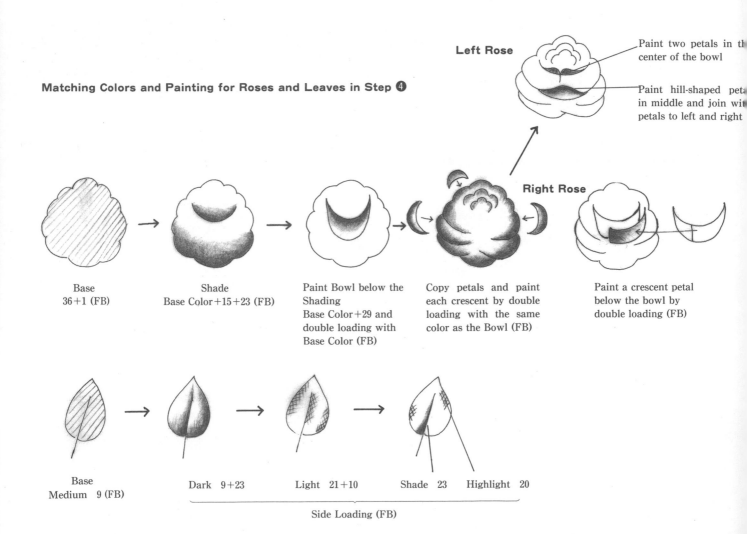

Left Rose

Paint two petals in the center of the bowl

Paint hill-shaped peta in middle and join wit petals to left and right

Matching Colors and Painting for Roses and Leaves in Step ❹

Right Rose

Base
36+1 (FB)

Shade
Base Color+15+23 (FB)

Paint Bowl below the
Shading
Base Color+29 and
double loading with
Base Color (FB)

Copy petals and paint
each crescent by double
loading with the same
color as the Bowl (FB)

Paint a crescent petal
below the bowl by
double loading (FB)

Base
Medium 9 (FB)

Dark 9+23

Light 21+10

Shade 23   Highlight 20

Side Loading (FB)

FRAME

from page 45

● Materials and Tools

Small Wooden Frame 23.6cm×19.2cm (9 1/4"×7 1/2")
Acrylic-based Water Paints
   Rose(2), Marine Green(10), Sky Blue(12), Pilot Blue(13), Golden Brown(19), White(26),
   Burgundy(36), Niagara Green(37), Navy(38)
Brushes BF,FB,RB,LB,
Medium for Waterproofs the base
Water-based Varnish for non-glossy finish

● Instructions

❶ Prepare materials. (Refer to page 8)
❷ Paint the base with 12+37 (BF).
❸ Paint Pink and Blue flowers in order as in the diagram
❹ Paint small chrysanthemums as in the diagram.
❺ Lightly paint chrysanthemum buds with 26 mixed with water (RB). Paint leaves using S
  strokes with 10 (FB).
❻ Finish up. (Refer to page 11)

Color Matching Chart for Blue and Pink Flowers

	Shade	Dark	Medium	Light	Highlight
Blue Flowers	Dark Color+38	13+38	13	13+26	26
Pink Flowers	36	2+36	2	2+26	26

Painting Blue and Pink Flowers in Step ❸

Base
Medium Color (FB)   Dark Color Light Color   Shade   Highlight   Outline with
               Side Loading (FB)   Side Loading (FB)   Highlight Color (LB)

Color Matching for Small Chrysanthemums in step ❹

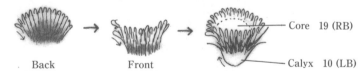

Back   Front   Core 19 (RB)
                             Calyx 10 (LB)

Paint carefully one by one by
double loading edge of a flat brush
with 26 and 10 pushing from top to
bottom (FB)

[Actual Size]

Left and Right

Top and Bottom

HEART-SHAPED GIFT BOX

from page 48

●Materials and Tools

Beige Heart-Shaped Paper Box 16.5cm×14cm (6 1/2"×5 1/2"), depth 10cm (4")
Acylic-based Water Paints
    Vandyke Brown(22), White(26), Polar Bear(28)
Brushes BF,FB,RB,LB

●Instructions

❶ Paint flowers in five places; on the middle of lid and sides. Add water to 22 and paint lightly (BF).
❷ Transfer the pattern. (Refer to page 9)
❸ Paint base for roses with 28 mixed with water. Paint petals one by one by double loading with 26 and 28 (FB). Paint comma strokes and
   small flowers around the flower (RB).
❹ Paint leaves the same way as the flowers, by double loading (FB). Paint stems (LB).
❺ Shade around flowers and leaves with 22 (FB).
❻ Paint lines with 22 around and underneath the lid (LB). Paint leaves using S strokes with 22 (FB).
❼ Paint 1 cm (3/8") checker pattern around the lid (FB).

[Actual Size]

ROUND GIFT BOX
from page 48

● Materials and Tools

Dark Green Round Paper Box diameter 24cm (9 1/2"), depth 15cm (6")
Acrylic-based Water Paints
  Highland Green(9), Marine Green(10), Dusky Purple(15), Bronze Yellow(21), Vandyke Brown(22), Black(23), White(26), Alizalin(27),
  Polar Bear(28), Opaline Green(29), Old Rose(33), Flax(34), Magnolia(35), Burgundy(36), Navy(38), Taupe(39)
Brushes FB,BF,LB, Stencil Brush(Fine),Stylus

● Instructions

❶ Tranfer the pattern in four places on the lid and side. (Refer to page 9) Copy lace pattern onto side after painting flowers.

❷ Paint the roses in the order shown in the separate chart.

❸ Paint the leaves in the shadows of other leaves with 23, paint with the same color matching for leaves as in the Lamp Shade on page 82 (FB).

❹ Paint bouquet around roses with the same color matching as in step ⑤ of the Lamp Shade, tap the base with 9+38, and paint the flowers on this with 26 (FB).

❺ Paint ribbon in the same order as in the separate chart.

❻ Paint the lace with C strokes by side loading with 26.
Paint lightly inside the lace with 26 thinned with water (FB).
Paint the patterns with comma strokes (RB), and paint dots around this (Stylus).

❼ Paint the dead branch around the lid using any or all of the colors 39, 22, or 28 by drawing the brush along the lid (RB). Paint lace on the sides as well.

❽ Paint 1.5cm (5/8") wide check pattern on the sides of the lid with 39 and 22, taking care not to mix the colors (FB).

Color Matching Chart

	Shade	Dark Color	Medium Color	Light Color	Highlight Color
Middle Rose	23	36+15	36+27	Medium+33	Light+29
Left Rose	23	Medium+15+23	35+33	Medium+29	Light+28
Right Rose	23	Medium+15+23	35+15+36	Medium+28	Light+26
Leaves	23	Medium+23	10+21+34	Medium+34	Light+34
Ribbon	23	Medium+15	26+33+15	Medium+26	26

Painting Roses in step ❷ (FB)

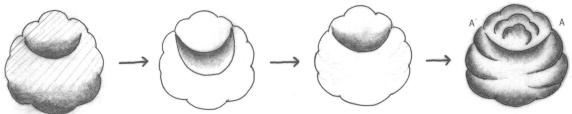

Copy outline of the pattern, paint base Medium Color, paint lower part of bud by side loading larger with Dark Color

Double load with Medium Color and Light Color and paint crescents

Side load onto crescent with Shade

Copy the petals, paint crescents by side loading with Light Color and Medium Color. Join petals A' and A together. Finally, paint outline of petals with Highlight Color (LB).

Painting Ribbon in step ❺ (Use only FB)

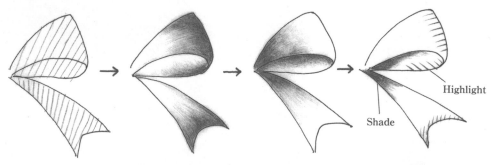

Paint base with Medium Color

Side load with Light Color

Side load with Dark Color

Side load with Shade and Highlight Color

PILL BOX, HEART DECORATION

from page 49

●Materials and Tools

Wooden Pill Box diameter 5.7 cm (2 1/4")
Wooden Heart (Puffed Heart)
6cm ×5.7cm (2 1/2"×2 1/4")
Acrylic-based Water Paints
 Claret(3), Highland Green(9),
 Marine Green(10), Dusky Purple(15),
 Yellow Ochre(20), Blonze Yellow(21),
 Black(23), White(26), Alizarin(27),
 Opaline Green(29), Old Rose(33),
 Burgundy(36), Navy(38)
Brushes BF,FB,RB,LB, Stencil Brush(Fine)
Medium for Waterproofs the base
Water-based Varnish for non-glossy finish

●Instructions

❶ Prepare materials. (Refer to page 8)

❷ Paint base with 3+26 (BF).

❸ Paint roses the same way as the middle round flower in the Round Gift Box on page 86.

❹ Use base Pink for the rose bud, shade one side with 36, and highlight the other side by side loading with 26 (FB).

❺ Paint the bouquet the same way as in step ⑤ of the Lamp Shade on page 82, tap the base with 9+38 and paint the flower on top of this with 26.

❻ Refer to the Frame on page 84 and paint the small chrysanthemum.

❼ Refer to the Lamp Shade on page 82 and paint the leaves. Paint the frame for the rose buds with 10+23 alternately light and dark (RB)

❽ Finish up. (Refer to page 11)

[Actual Size]

PLATE
pages 20 and 21

Vege tables and Kitchen Parts

●Materials and Tools

Turned Wooden Plate (flat) diameter 30.5 cm (12")
Acrylic-based Water Paints
 Strawberry(4), Brilliant Yellow(7), Scarlet(5), Marine Green(10), Vandyke Brown(22), White(26)
Brushes BF,RB
Acrylic Wood Stain(Charcal)

●Instructions

❶ Put a small amount of Acrylic Wood Stain onto a towel and press into the inside edge of the plate (between the leaves and the Red Brown line).

❷ Paint the edge of the plate with Salmon Pink (BF).

❸ Transfer the pattern. (Refer to page 9) Rotate the pattern and transfer the other half of the pattern.

❹ Paint the base for the kitchen parts Cream. Shade with Cream+22.

❺ Paint the tops of the mushrooms Maroon. Paint the backs of the tops and bases Beige. Paint lines on the shade and backs of tops with 22.

❻ Paint the base for the carrots Orange, shade with Orange+22.

88

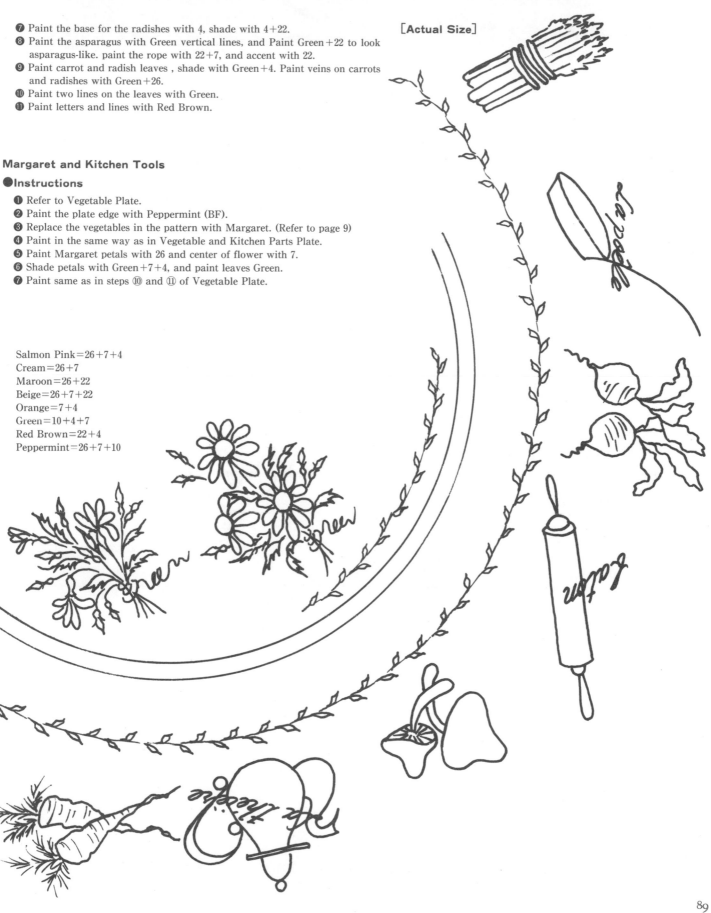

❼ Paint the base for the radishes with 4, shade with 4+22.

❽ Paint the asparagus with Green vertical lines, and Paint Green+22 to look asparagus-like. paint the rope with 22+7, and accent with 22.

❾ Paint carrot and radish leaves , shade with Green+4. Paint veins on carrots and radishes with Green+26.

❿ Paint two lines on the leaves with Green.

⓫ Paint letters and lines with Red Brown.

[Actual Size]

Margaret and Kitchen Tools

●Instructions

❶ Refer to Vegetable Plate.

❷ Paint the plate edge with Peppermint (BF).

❸ Replace the vegetables in the pattern with Margaret. (Refer to page 9)

❹ Paint in the same way as in Vegetable and Kitchen Parts Plate.

❺ Paint Margaret petals with 26 and center of flower with 7.

❻ Shade petals with Green+7+4, and paint leaves Green.

❼ Paint same as in steps ❿ and ⓫ of Vegetable Plate.

Salmon Pink＝26+7+4
Cream＝26+7
Maroon＝26+22
Beige＝26+7+22
Orange＝7+4
Green＝10+4+7
Red Brown＝22+4
Peppermint＝26+7+10

OVAL BOX

from page 21

●Materials and Tools

Oval Wooden Cheese Box 16.1cm×20.2cm (6 1/2"×8"), height 8.6cm (3 1/4")
Acrylic-based Water Paints
   Strawberry(4), Billiant Yellow(7), Marine Green(10), Oxford Blue(14), Vandyke Brown(22), White(26)
Brushes BF,RB

●Instructions

❶ Paint base for all except the rim of the lid Cream (BF).
❷ Cover outside of the box with masking tape, leaving gaps of 5 mm (1/4") and paint Red Brown stripes. Paint sides of lid same color (BF).
❸ Hold the four corners of the sponge, dip into Salmon Pink , remove excess paint, and tap onto lid.
❹ Transfer the pattern. (Refer to page 9)
❺ Paint face and hands and legs with Sunset. Paint nose, cheeks, arms and legs with Sunset+19.
❻ Paint outline from step ⑤, eyes, mouth, mustache with Sunset+22.
❼ Paint base for hair with 7, shade with Golden Brown.
❽ Paint base for hat, clothes, pants, and cooking tray with Gray. Shade with Dark Brown. Paint stripes, buttons, and shoes. Highlight with Gray+26.
❾ Paint White part of base for apron, jacket and hat with 26. Shade with Golden Brown.
❿ Paint red base for scarf and necktie with 4, shade with 4+14.
⓫ Paint wine bottle with 10+22, label with 26+7+22, and paint letters and cork with Golden Brown.
⓬ Paint base for frying pan with Golden Brown. Shade with Golden Brown+22.
⓭ Paint letters with Red Brown.

Cream＝26+7
Red Brown＝22+4
Salmon Pink＝26+7+4
Sunset＝26+7+4
      (a little more 26 than in Salmon Pink)
Gray＝26+22+14
Dark Brown＝14+22
Golden Brown＝7+22

[Actual Size]

CHRISTMAS TREE

from page 52

●Materials and Tools

Wooden Christmas Tree 32cm (12 3/4"), tall 32cm (12 3/4)
Acrylic-based Water Paints
   Strawberry(4), Billiant Yellow(7), Marine Green(10), Oxford Blue(14), Dusky Purple(15), Vandyke Brown(22), White(26)
Brushes RB
Acrylic Wood Stain(Charcoal)

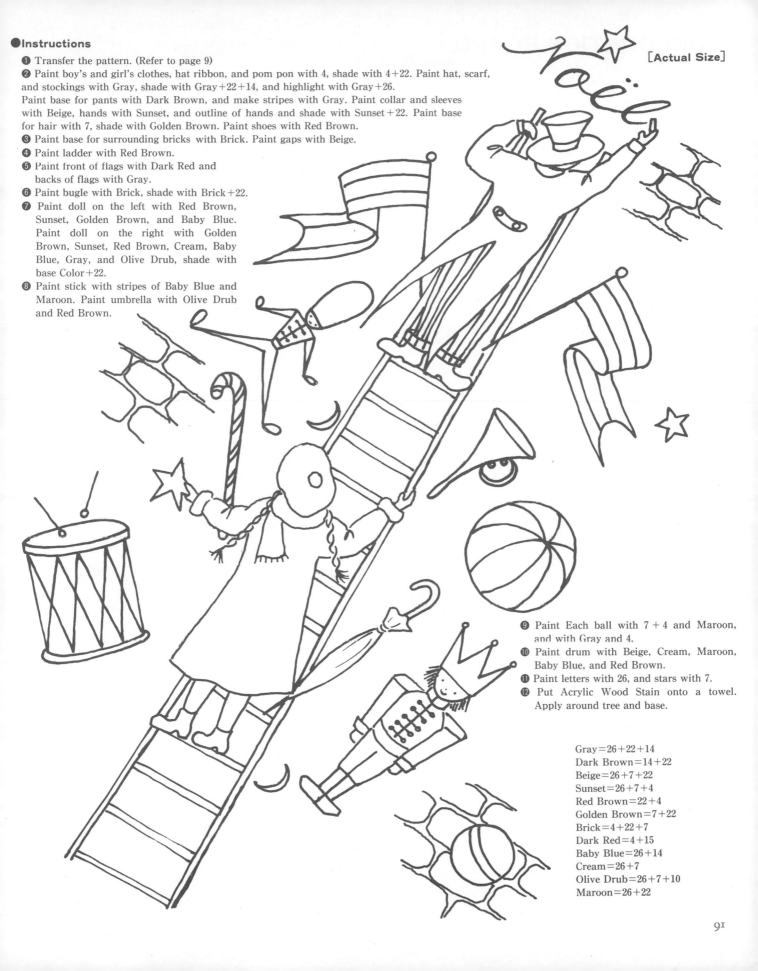

●Instructions

❶ Transfer the pattern. (Refer to page 9)

❷ Paint boy's and girl's clothes, hat ribbon, and pom pon with 4, shade with 4+22. Paint hat, scarf, and stockings with Gray, shade with Gray+22+14, and highlight with Gray+26.
Paint base for pants with Dark Brown, and make stripes with Gray. Paint collar and sleeves with Beige, hands with Sunset, and outline of hands and shade with Sunset+22. Paint base for hair with 7, shade with Golden Brown. Paint shoes with Red Brown.

❸ Paint base for surrounding bricks with Brick. Paint gaps with Beige.

❹ Paint ladder with Red Brown.

❺ Paint front of flags with Dark Red and backs of flags with Gray.

❻ Paint bugle with Brick, shade with Brick+22.

❼ Paint doll on the left with Red Brown, Sunset, Golden Brown, and Baby Blue. Paint doll on the right with Golden Brown, Sunset, Red Brown, Cream, Baby Blue, Gray, and Olive Drub, shade with base Color+22.

❽ Paint stick with stripes of Baby Blue and Maroon. Paint umbrella with Olive Drub and Red Brown.

[Actual Size]

❾ Paint Each ball with 7 + 4 and Maroon, and with Gray and 4.

❿ Paint drum with Beige, Cream, Maroon, Baby Blue, and Red Brown.

⓫ Paint letters with 26, and stars with 7.

⓬ Put Acrylic Wood Stain onto a towel. Apply around tree and base.

Gray＝26＋22＋14
Dark Brown＝14＋22
Beige＝26＋7＋22
Sunset＝26＋7＋4
Red Brown＝22＋4
Golden Brown＝7＋22
Brick＝4＋22＋7
Dark Red＝4＋15
Baby Blue＝26＋14
Cream＝26＋7
Olive Drub＝26＋7＋10
Maroon＝26＋22

DECORATION BOARD

from page 53

●Materials and Tools

Wooden Welcome Board
45cm×23.6cm (17 3/4"×9 1/4")
Acrylic-based Water Pains
  Strawberry(4), Billiant Yellow(7), Marine Green(10),
  Oxford Blue(14),Vandyke Brown(22), White(26)
Brushes RB
Acrylic Wood
Stain(Charcal)

●Instructions

❶ Transfer only the center line of the cedar branch surrounding the pattern. (Refer to page 9)
❷ Dip a towel into Acrylic Wood Stain and apply outside of the line that has just been copied.
❸ Paint base inside of the line with Cream.
❹ When copying the pattern, be careful not to blur the border line that has just been painted.
❺ Paint cedar branch with Green+22.
❻ Refer to the Christmas Tree on pages 90 and 91 and paint the boy and girl.
❼ Paint front of flags with 4, 26, Navy Blue, and backs with Gray. Paint poles with Red Brown
❽ Paint base for scrolls with Cream, shade by mixing with 7, 10 and 22.

[Actual Size]

⑨ Color the base for the stick canes Golden Brown, and add stripes with Beige. Paint base for umbrella Golden Brown, paint shade and handle with Golden Brown+22.

⑩ For the dolls on the left and right, paint the hat and crown Golden Brown, clothes Dark Brown and Red Brown+7, shade with 22+Base Color, highlight with 26.

⑪ Paint stockings Golden Brown and Dark Brown, drums Golden Brown, Cream, and Red Brown, and paint lines with Dark Brown.

⑫ Paint bugle and ball with Dark Brown and Beige.

⑬ Paint base for stars with 7, shade and outline with 7+22.

⑭ Hold four corners of sponge and dip into darker Cream Color than the Base Color and tap around the positions for the letters. Tap Salmon Pink inside this.

⑮ Paint letters with Red Brown

Cream=26+7
Salmon Pink=26+4+7
Green=10+4+7
Navy Blue=14+22
Gray=26+22+14
Red Brown=22+4
Golden Brown=7+22
Beige=26+7+22
Dark Brown=14+22
Sunset=26+7+4
(a little more 26 than in Salmon Pink)

HOUSE-SHAPED TISSUE BOX

from page 53

●Materials and Tools

House-Shaped Wooden Tissue Box 16.7cm×16.2cm (6 1/2"×6 1/4") height 22cm (8 3/4")
Acrylic-based Water Paints
   Strawberry(4), Brilliant Yellow(7), Marine Green(10), Oxford Blue(14), Vandyke Brown(22), White(26)
Brushes BF,RB
Acrylic Wood Stain(Charcal)

●Instructions

❶ Transfer the pattern onto the sides of the house. (Refer to page 9) Copy only the bricks onto the sides of the house that can not be seen in the photo.

❷ Paint the base for the bricks and arch stones with Cream. Mix Base Color with Golden Brown, Beige, Orange, and 22.

❸ Paint the girl's face and legs with Sunset, and outline with Sunset+22. Paint hat and gloves with 4, shade with 4+22. Paint hair with Golden Brown and highlight hat with same color. Paint scarf with Gray, and stripe with Red Brown. Paint jacket with Cream, skirt with Dark Brown, and base for boots with Red Brown. Add 22 to Base Color and shade.

❹ Paint base for dog with Cream, shade with Cream+7+22. Paint eyes with 22. Paint stockings with Baby Blue. Outline with 22 and add stripes.

❺ Paint cedar branches in the arch with Green and Green+22, add letters with Red Brown.

❻ Paint base for stockings with Gray, Orange, and Cream. Paint stripes and patterns with 4, Red Brown and Green. Paint openings for stockings with Base Color+22. Paint rope and clips with Red Brown.

❼ After painting, lightly paint the wall and back with Golden Brown thinned with water.

❽ Paint base for the chimney with Cream, and the roof Baby Blue. Partially overlap with Golden Brown. Copy the patterns for the bricks and paint.

❾ Place a small amount of Acrylic Wood Stain onto a cloth and press onto the roof and corners of the wall.

[Actual Size]

Cream＝26＋7
Golden Brown＝7＋22
Beige＝26＋7＋22
Orange＝7＋4
Sunset＝26＋7＋4
Gray＝26＋22＋14
Red Brown＝22＋4
Dark Brown＝14＋22
Baby Blue＝16＋14

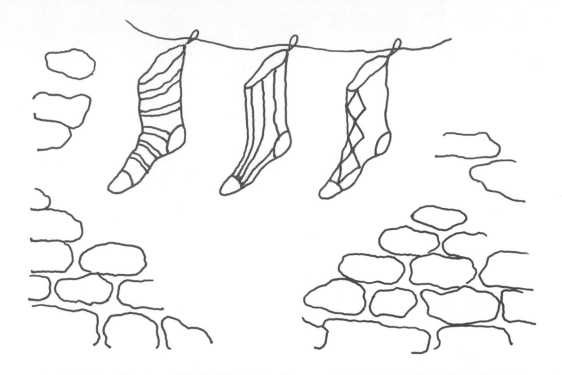

[Actual Size]

GIFT CAN
from page 53

● Materials and Tools

Open Can height 14cm (5 1/2"), 11cm (4 1/4"), 7.5cm (3")
Acrylic-based Water Paints
   Strawberry(4), Brilliant Yellow(7), Marine Green(10), Oxford Blue(14), Dusky Purple(15),
   Vandyke Brown(22), White(26)
Brushes BF,RB
Medium for Waterproofs the base
Water-based Varnish for non-glossy finish

● Instructions

❶ Prepare materials (Refer to page 8).

❷ Paint the main portion with Color A (Refer to- descriptions of each craft), lid with 22+15 (BF).

❸ Copy only one line from the cedar branch surrounding the pattern (Refer to page 9).

❹ Paint inside the line with Color B (BF). Hold the four corners of a sponge, dip into Color C, remove excess, and tap onto Color B.

❺ Paint each animal (Refer to descriptions of each craft).

❻ Paint cedar wreath with Green and Green+22. Paint base for berries with 4, shade with 4+ 15. Paint the holly leaves and berries the same way. Paint base for Yule logs with Golden Brown, shade with 22, highlight with 26. Paint base for scroll with 26, shade with 26+7+ 22, outline with 22.

❼ Finish up. (Refer to page 11)

Small Bird

A=26+7 B=Light Salmon Pink
C=Dark Salmon Pink
Paint base for small bird with 26+7, shade with 7 + 4 and 22, and paint eyes and legs with 22.
Paint base for birdhouse with Golden Brown, wood grain with 22+14, and shade with 22.
Green=10+4+7
Golden Brown=7+22
Salmon Pink=26+7+4
Red Brown=22+4

[Actual Size]

Rabbit

A = 26+7+22   B = Light Salmon Pink
C = Dark Salmon Pink
Paint a base of 26+22 for the rabbit. Shade by
adding 22 to the base color and add the eye.
Paint Salmon Pink on the ear. Paint the grass
with Green and Green+7.

Squirrel

A = 26+10+7   B = 26+7   C = Salmon Pink
Paint the base in Golden Brown. Shade and
paint the eye with Red Brown.

[Actual Size]

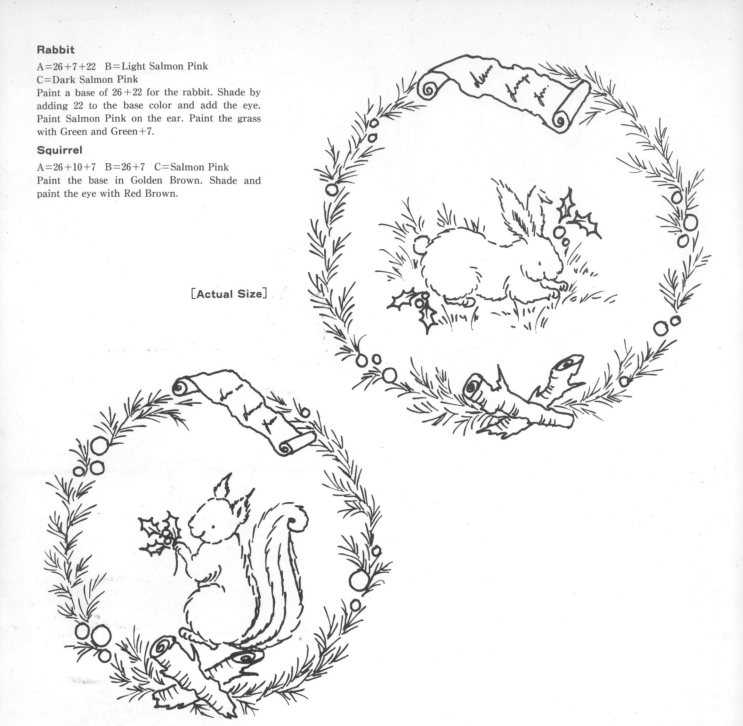